PROFILING MACHINES

The MIT Press, Cambridge, Massachusetts, London, England

Mapping the Personal Information Economy

PROFILING MACHINES

Greg Elmer

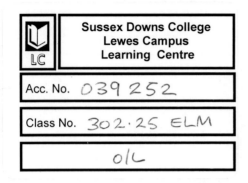
This book was set in Bembo and Meta by Asco Typesetters, Hong Kong, and was printed and bound in the United States of America.

Library of Congress Cataloging-in-Publication Data

Elmer, Greg, 1967–
   Profiling machines : mapping the personal information economy / Greg Elmer.
      p.   cm.
   Includes bibliographical references and index.
   ISBN 0-262-05073-0 (hc. : alk. paper)
   1. Consumer profiling. 2. Privacy, Right of. I. Title: Personal information economy. II. Title.
HF5415.32.E488   2004
658.8′34—dc21   2003056148

For all her love, courage, and strength, this book is dedicated to Paula Gardner.

CONTENTS

Portions of this book were presented at a number of academic conferences and colloquia, which provided wonderful opportunities to refine the arguments presented here. Many of the theoretical arguments discussed in chapter 2 were first presented at Eighty-fourth Annual Convention of the National Communication Association in New York City (November 21–24, 1998) and at the First Annual Conference of the Association of Internet Researchers in Lawrence, Kansas (September 14–17, 2000). Portions of chapter 6 were presented at the Third Annual Conference of the Association of Internet Researchers in Maastricht, The Netherlands (October 13–16, 2002), and at the University of Vienna.

ACKNOWLEDGMENTS

Chapter 2 first appeared in the journal *New Media and Society*. Earlier versions of chapters 3 and 4 appeared, respectively, in *Convergence: A Journal of Research into New Media Technologies* and in *Topia: A Canadian Journal of Cultural Studies*. Chapter 5 is a much revised version of a paper first published by *Space and Culture*. And portions of chapter 6 were initially published in my edited volume *Critical Perspectives on the Internet* (Rowman & Littlefield, 2002).

As a project that has spanned a number of years, this book would not have been published without the help of family and many colleagues, students, mentors, and friends. For an infinite number of reasons, I'm first and foremost indebted to my doctoral advisor, Briankle Chang. My doctoral committee members—Henry Geddes, Justin Lewis, and Robert Schwartzwald—also deserve my gratitude.

A number of colleagues have read or reviewed this manuscript or otherwise provided me with guidance. I am particularly indebted to Mark Andrejevic, Elfriede Fursich, Steve Jones, Richard Rogers, and Rob Shields for their engaging exchanges and close readings of various chapters. Many others have directly or indirectly influenced my thinking on issues of surveillance, new information and communication technologies, computer profiling, and contemporary cultural theory. I'd like to thank Bram Abramson, Jody Berland, Nick Dyer-Witheford, Katya Haskins, David Lyon, Toby Miller, Brian M. Murphy, Greg Seigworth, Jennifer Slack, Jonathan Sterne, Fred Turner, and Greg Wise and for their unique contributions.

The anonymous reviewers from the MIT Press were of immense help in offering suggestions for improvements, many of which have been incorporated into the book. A debt of gratitude also goes to my editor, Doug Sery, who was supportive and encouraging from the earliest stages of this project.

For logistical and institutional support, I'd like to thank my research assistants, Timothy Moriarty and Ryan Ellis; Florida State University communication department chair Stephen McDowell; and dean John Mayo.

This book would, of course, never have seen the light of day without the encouragement and love of my family, Paula, Keegan, and Lilianna, and my parents, Chris and Carol Elmer.

PROFILING MACHINES

1

As we begin the new millennium, theories of government, citizenship, and even "representation" are coming under intense scrutiny. The demise of the cold war and the subsequent rise in separatist, ethnic, religious, and terrorist politics have focused much attention on the reconfiguration of social spaces and the new geopolitical order. Such territorial matters are made all the more complex by the rapid colonization of outer space (through telecommunications and weather and military surveillance satellites) and cyberspace (through both the Internet and intranets), the ongoing deregulation and decentralization of Western industrial state apparatuses, and the overwhelming predominance of the market. As a consequence, established definitions of *nation, state,*

THE CULTURE AND TECHNOLOGIES OF PROFILING

territory, citizenship, and *consumption*—all fundamental tropes of modernity—have been called into question. Thus, at a time when researchers and political pundits continue to discuss the dwindling opportunities for citizens to have their voices heard by government, consumers are increasingly "solicited" for their opinions and desires by geographically ubiquitous consumer feedback technologies.

Taking such technological, topographical, and political changes into consideration, *Profiling Machines: Mapping the Personal Information Economy* attempts to supplement the dearth of ideological and textual critiques of consumer culture in media and cultural studies with a technological and topographical understanding of consumer profiling, solicitation, feedback, and mapping technologies—highlighting the manner in which "consuming places" (Urry 1995) also serve as key sites of automated demographic solicitations. The analysis of prevalent trends in commercial and popular iconography (on screen, in print, or on strategically placed billboards) is placed within a digitized and networked information economy that increasingly requires consumers to exchange demographic and psychographic information for commodities and services.

In an era where two-thirds of all commercial campaigns ask for some degree of feedback from consumers (via sweepstakes entry forms, bar-coded discount cards, special club enrollment forms, online membership forms, and so on) (Woodside 1994, 26), the lack of any sustained critique of the topography of the new economy of consumption is startling. Based on its title, Andrew Wernick's *Promotional Culture: Advertising, Ideology, and Symbolic Expression* (1991) seems to promise a study of the relationship between images, marketing campaigns, and emerging feedback techniques and networks. Although he recognizes a broader playing field and system of production, Wernick (1991, vii) (like many of his peers in the fields of media and cultural studies) restricts his analysis to the textual and ideological aspects of the visual image:

> Promotion (my term for advertising and its practices taken in the widest and most generic sense) was a rhetorical form diffused throughout our culture. As such, it had come to shape not only that culture's symbolic and ideological contents, but also its ethos, texture, and constitution as a whole.

The lack of a critical body of literature on the topography of consumer feedback technologies is not limited to the fields of media and cultural studies. *Profiling Machines* argues that recent studies on information "surveillance" also continue to downplay the important spatial and architectural dynamics of consumer-profiling technologies and examines (1) the increasing intransigence of consumer feedback techniques in digital and multimedia and (2) the increasingly routinized practices of consumer feedback techniques in everyday life, offering the raw materials for simulated maps of consumer markets.

Theoretically, this book focuses on debates surrounding Michel Foucault's (1977) panoptic, "all-seeing" model of surveillance. Arguing for a "diagrammatic" method for studying both consuming spaces and consumer profiling and feedback technologies, the book rethinks Foucault's institutional and architectural framework through Gilles Deleuze's (1992a) thoughts on the circulation of information in decentralized "societies of control." In so doing, the book attempts to connect the practices of everyday consumption with a broad information apparatus that forecasts and simulates sociospatial relationships and new media capabilities.

The term *surveillance* does not adequately capture the multiplicity of processes that *request* data by surveying and monitoring consumers and also by automatically collecting, storing, and cross-referencing consumers' personal information with a complex array of other market data (such as production, distribution, and sales data). Nor does the term *surveillance* alone seem to capture the social significance of *requiring* the divulgence of personal information as a precondition for using new information and communication technologies such as digital television and the World Wide Web. Ultimately, what both requesting and requiring personal information highlight is the centrality of producing, updating, and deploying consumer *profiles*—simulations or pictures of consumer likes, dislikes, and behaviors that are automated within the process of consuming goods, services, or media and that increasingly anticipate our future needs and wants based on our aggregated past choices and behaviors. And although Foucault warns of the self-disciplinary model of punishment in panoptic surveillance, computer profiling, conversely, oscillates between seemingly rewarding participation and punishing attempts to elect not to divulge personal information. This blurring of punishments and rewards—subtle *requests* and not so subtle *commands* for personal information—is a reoccurring problematic in both social critiques and popular (fictional) treatments of consumer profiling.

THE PROFILING GAME: INTERTEXTUALITY AND INSTRUMENTALITY

In the Hollywood motion picture *The Game*, Michael Douglas is again cast as an unpleasant, arrogant, and unprincipled business executive. Perhaps more than any other actor, Douglas's on-screen persona or filmography—as evidenced in the motion pictures *Wall Street*, *Falling Down*, *Fatal Attraction*, *Basic Instinct*, *Disclosure*, and *The Perfect Murder*—has elicited strong reactions from members of various social groups who are troubled by his films' representations of female sexuality, business ethics, race relations, and sexual harassment (Gabriel 1996; Davies 1995; Holmlund 1991). Typecast in similar roles over the years, Douglas has developed an on-screen *profile*—the culmination or composite of many of his roles —of male victim, white vigilante, and corporate devil that often comments on contested areas of American political life. Douglas's career has in some part shaped the popular imagination of the entrepreneurial excesses of post-Reagan individualism and the increasingly complex dynamics of race, sex, and class identity politics.

As an individual text, *The Game* also engages a quite different definition of profiling. The film begins with a now familiar Douglas character—rich, brash, and obnoxious—receiving a mysterious "customized adventure" birthday present from his estranged younger brother. Later, as Douglas's character, Nicholas Van Orton, inquires about his gift at the adventure company's office, he is unaware that by volunteering to answer a series of questions and perform a battery of simulations and tests that are meant to elicit his consumption patterns, personal habits, finances, and physical attributes, he has already started the "game." The film's suspense is subsequently sustained by the viewer's inability to determine whether the adventure company has cheated Van Orton or has hypercustomized an intensely thrilling game. In other words, the audience is left wondering whether the company has solicited Van Orton's profile to customize and enhance his adventure or whether it has done so to gain access to his many password-protected sources of wealth. In keeping with the conventions of the action genre, Van Orton and his female sidekick/ love interest face a number of seemingly life-threatening scenarios. Consequently, as the game becomes exponentially intense and seemingly dangerous, Van Orton becomes increasingly incapable of distinguishing fact and fiction. Unable to determine whether he is indeed playing a game, the protagonist is slowly but surely stripped of both his identity and institutional forms of identification.

Thus, viewers first believe that Van Orton's profiling has resulted in severe *punishment,* but his subsequent abduction to a third-world shanty town eventually leads to a deeply spiritual *reward*—the ultimate goal of the brother's gift adventure. As the game challenges Van Orton's sense of self and value, he begins to undergo a transformation—by renouncing his narcissistic personality and actualizing his well-intentioned, benevolent "real" self.

Although *The Game*'s conclusion conforms to Hollywood's need for happy endings, it also champions the (self-)revolutionary and spiritual power of consumer-profiling technologies—the ability of hypercustomized products and services to unearth the real self.

Despite the film's romantic ending, *The Game* offers a telling account of the potential effects of divulging personal information. On the one hand, consumers face the fear and punishment of losing their virtual identities by having credit-card or Social Security numbers stolen or otherwise appropriated for purposes not of their own choosing, and on the other hand, consumers enjoy the ultimate convenience of being offered products and services that are "profiled" to their individual tastes. What's more, given the ubiquity and complexity of today's personal-information economy, initial "rewards" (such as free T-shirts for credit-card applications) can easily later turn into "punishments" (such as junk mail, irritating phone solicitations, identity fraud, and compromised and damaged credit). Such rewards and punishments of consumer profiling indicate the continuous and increasing attempts of producers to improve both quantitatively and qualitatively their consumer "intelligence" gathering—to track and integrate the everyday behavior of consumers into other production, sales, and distribution data.

Michael Douglas's general on-screen profile is not the same as his character in *The Game*, who is subject to the sort of consumer profiling described above in the introduction to the film. But the actor's persona or life's work is condensed (or thematized), named ("angry white guy"), and consequently "read" against—or in conjunction with—various social and political phenomena (such as sexual harassment or affirmative action). In the field of media and cultural studies, Tony Bennett and Janet Woollacott's *Bond and Beyond: The Political Career of a Popular Hero* (1987, 45) conceptualizes this first definition of profiling as "intertextual" relationships—"the social organisation of the relations between texts within specific conditions of reading." John Tulloch and Manuel Alvarado's (1983, 2) study of the long-running British science fiction television series *Doctor Who* likewise discusses the text as an "extensive" phenomenon, which for the authors means in conjunction with "industrial, institutional, narrative, generic, and professional" practices "existing outside the programme."

In the second definition, however, profiling is discussed as an instrumental and economic[1] process that focuses on the collection, storage, networking, diagnosis, and deployment of demographic and psychographic information. This kind of profiling is broadly defined as an ongoing distribution and cataloguing of information about the desires, habits, and location of individuals and groups. This instrumental approach is, in other words, much more concerned with segmenting, rationalizing, and predicting consumer behavior—what Toby Miller (1997) characterizes as "distributional politics"—than with "reading" or tracing the trajectories of overlapping texts. However, since instrumental profiles (such as the "soccer mom," which was constructed by American political party pollsters and campaign researchers to target swing voters) also tend to dominate intertextual political and consumer discourse (from television news to advertisements for minivans), textual and instrumental approaches to profiling seem to offer complementary perspectives (see chapter 2 for a theoretical discussion of panopticism and synopticism).

Thus, in lieu of focusing exclusively on the *dominant trends* in commercial iconography, advertising, and consumer culture that tend to end with questions of textual "representation" (are we in this picture?), this book highlights the process of attempting to avoid, redress, or otherwise account for the *failure* of producers to capture an audience, market, or consumer. In other words, the book examines the means (namely, the techniques and technologies) by which niche markets are targeted, customized, and rationalized. It focuses on the role that automated solicitations of consumer choices (at the cash register, video store, automatic teller machine, Web, and so on) and subsequent simulated maps play in the larger enterprise of *forecasting* market shifts and formatting

topographies of consumption (whether in urban and rural landscapes or in cyberspace).

CULTURAL STUDIES OF SPACE

As a study of the geographical and virtual aspects of consumer
profiling, this book continues the interdisciplinary tradition of
critical geography, history, communication, cultural theory, and
political economy that was forged in the scholarship of Henri
Lefebvre (1991), Harold Innis (1972, 1951), David Harvey (1989),
and James Carey (1989), among others. A few words about their
seminal contributions might therefore help frame the context
within which I discuss consumer profiling in the so-called information age.

The reassertion of issues of space into critical cultural theory, as Ed
Soja (1996) describes it, is a surprisingly recent phenomenon in
communication studies. There are at least four reasons why topographical questions have recently problematized our understanding
of communication and media. First, new information technologies
(beginning with the telegraph in the late nineteenth century and
continuing most recently to satellite, Internet, and intranet networks) have challenged our terrestrial definitions of space itself and
extended our understanding of space to the realms of outer space
and cyberspace. Second, the fragmentation of the body politic and
the increased importance of social movements have led cultural
theorists to turn to places of inhabitation to ground the complex
power dynamics of identity politics. Third, on a larger scale, issues
of space have been tied to the development of a global economy
and global culture. And finally, the breakup of cold-war geopolitical formations and the reemergence of ethnic and religious
nationalism in many parts of the world have led many to question
the stability of national states and territorial borders.

As is customary with most critical and cultural approaches to social phenomena, Karl Marx provides a useful framework for discussing topographical questions, even though he was relatively silent on the issue of space and geography. The Marxist perspective, in other words, is overwhelmingly shaped by events in the temporal plane —the historical periodization of the transition from capitalism to socialism, the creation of surplus value from time "added on" to the work day, and so on. In *Postmodern Geographies: The Reassertion of Space in Critical Social Theory* (1989), Edward Soja (1989) looks for the reasons for the resistance to issues of space in contemporary Western Marxism and finds three. First, Marx's only manuscript that directly engages issues of space, the *Grundrisse* (Outlines), was completed in 1857 but was not translated into German until the late 1950s or into English until the early 1970s. Second, Soja argues that Marx's theory of alienation is driven by the temporal workday. Finally, Marx's aversion to the Hegelian "spirit" is often linked to its status as a "plane" of existence, a place to be reached (Soja 1989, 46).

Henri Lefebvre, one of the first scholars to challenge the temporal bias of Marxism, nevertheless draws heavily from orthodox Marxism. For Lefebvre, both alienated labor and "abstract space" are removed from the experiences of the working class. Lefebvre's class revolution focuses on the production of "differentiated space" by both the working class and "minorities"—a space that is free from domination and exploitation.

Lefebvre's *The Production of Space* (1991)—an admittedly difficult and at times contradictory work—offers two general concepts that contribute important perspectives on the topographic study of personal information. First, in keeping with his view that all space is produced socially (through language, codes, or "designs" that bridge "mental" and physical space), Lefebvre (1991, 38–39) insists on the importance of spatial practices—the routines that produce locations and forge links between work and leisure. Consequently, Lefebvre (1991, 16) notes that

> The project I am outlining, however, does not aim to pro-duce a (or *the*) discourse on space, but rather to expose the actual production of space by bringing the various kinds of space and the modalities of their genesis together within a single theory.

Second, with respect to spaces themselves, Lefebvre (1991, 38) calls "representations of space" the plans and diagrams that fall under the power of engineers and planners. As is shown in this book, in the so-called information age, such "diagrams," maps, and plans require constant updating because of the accelerating speed of change in demographic, psychographic, and geographic data— that is, the raw materials used to profile consumers. According to David Harvey's *The Condition of Postmodernity* (1989), such machinic diagrams—or what some have referred to as *cybernetic* systems of production[2] (Robins & Webster 1988; Mosco 1996; Tomas 1995)—typify the transition from a Fordist to a post-Fordist economy in which linear modes of production (such as the production line) are replaced by fully integrated and net-worked production, distribution, and sales loops. This "flexible" mode of production thus resulted in the rationalization of pro-duction techniques from large-scale inventory management in Fordist economies to "just-in-time" inventory systems in the post-Fordist economy (Harvey 1989, 159).

Stemming from a like-minded interest in technologies of space and economy, the work of Harold Innis has likewise offered a pro-ductive framework for many political economists and theorists, albeit from the perspective of political administration and nation-alism. Schooled in Chicago but raised in Canada, Innis has been widely associated with a uniquely North American perspective.[3] Innis's main works (1951, 1972) are concerned largely with "nation-binding technologies" and (in his writing on ancient civilizations) the importance of "territorial management." Innis argues that communication technologies are either "time or space biased," the former favoring the dissemination of information over a long period of time and the latter favoring the dissemination of information across vast spaces. Throughout his life, Innis became increasingly concerned with technological monopolies—that is, societies that have a preponderance of time-biased technologies (such as a stone tablet or parchment paper) that are prone to the centralization of knowledge (for example, in the church). Conversely, Innis argues that a preponderance of space-biased technologies (such as the telegraph or the telephone) centralizes power and knowledge in large cities. Contemporary privacy advocates would extend Innis's concern with archives of knowledge to the consumer database.

Building on Innis's thoughts on the management of space and territory, James Carey (1989) has questioned the impact of the time-space collapse (the technological overcoming of geographical barriers) on the machinations of economic markets in the United States. For him, the United States in the late nineteenth century was a "space-binding culture" that was fixated on building a unified nation-state (as opposed to a time-binding culture that focused on the continuance of centralized traditions and knowledge). The telegraph serves as a unique example, Carey (1989, 203) rightly argues, in that its separation of communication from transportation "allowed communication to control physical processes actively. The early use of the telegraph in railroad signaling is an example: telegraph messages could control the physical switching of rolling stock, thereby multiplying the purposes and effectiveness of communication."

After the introduction of the telegraph, mercantilism would never be the same. Since the buyer might never actually meet the seller of a product, administrative systems and regulations were required to standardize and govern trading practices. A system of grading commodities (particularly perishable goods) followed. Moreover, the telegraph wrought a fundamental shift in the notion of speculation-as-geography (buying goods low in one place and transporting them to sell at a higher price in another location) to speculation-as-futures (investing money on the basis of crop possibilities as opposed to the crops themselves) (Carey 1989, 217–221). The space-binding exploits of the telegraph would also lead to changing practices in journalism, the demise of vernacular languages, and the growth of "national news."

Focusing on France, Germany, and England in the nineteenth and twentieth centuries, Armand Mattelart's *The Invention of Communication* (1996) similarly discusses the relationship between trade and transportation routes, communication networks, and the nation-state. Complementing the work of Carey, Mattelart is most interested in the governmental regulations, standards, and rules that resulted from the need to unite and manage the national territory. The most explicit forms of such management of the significant precursors to the personal information economy were early cartographic efforts in seventeenth-century France—attempts to accurately document and assess the boundaries and contours of the national terrain. The standardization of weights and measurements and the installation of the metric system in 1840 were just a few initial attempts at governing the vast territory of France. In contrast to Carey and Innis, though, Mattelart (1996) contributes a unique understanding to issues of technology and space by examining both the telegraph and the railway—the first networked system of communication and transportation. Mattelart outlines the process by which rail lines facilitated the transportation of rail carriages and carried electronic pulses whose disruption indicated a potential derailment further down the line. Thus, Mattelart (1996, 9) discusses the establishment of a national bureaucracy (defined by systems of control, inventory, communication, and transportation) as well as the power of an emerging governmental and technological network, a modern industrial precursor to the computerized information age.

THE INFORMATION SOCIETY: FLOW, NETWORKING, AND AUTOMATION

Although transportation and communication remain fundamental components of contemporary postindustrialized nation-states, the emergence of an "information society" has clearly challenged modern definitions of *production, representation,* and now even *space* itself. The term *information society,* widely attributed to the social scientist Fritz Machlup, stems from his comprehensive accounting of informational "wealth" in the United States, *The Production and Distribution of Knowledge in the United States* (1962). Machlup's study was the first to recognize the growth of information services in the economic sphere and to attempt to legitimate such production in terms of measurements such as the gross national product (GNP). Machlup thus set out to measure information production in education, the emerging computer and data industry, and other information-based sectors such as law and insurance. Although Machlup's work is still widely respected today, his limited "measured" economic approach to information and knowledge production has come under intensified scrutiny. In Frank Webster's (1995) survey of the information society and its theoretical foundations, for instance, knowledge production is defined by increasingly more pervasive technological innovations such as the economic growth of the information sector, the changing dynamics of work and occupations, the collapse of spatial barriers, and the cultural impact of new technologies.

Speaking to the changing conventions in television programming, the British cultural theorist Raymond Williams perhaps unintentionally offered a defining characteristic of the coming information age. Williams recalled that the most striking aspect of American culture was the overwhelming preponderance of television commercials (or *adverts* in the British vernacular). Such program interruptions were initially considered by Williams (1974) to be highly fragmented and disjointed products—much like the components prior to a Taylorist assembly.

On consideration, though, Williams soon considered such texts to be highly organized units in the wider televisual economy. Focusing on the beginning and end of programs, Williams (1974, 89–96) began to detail the numerous devices used by television programmers to construct a sense of continuity or flow. The object of such a strategy was to maintain audience share. The insertion of a voiceover (on top of a concluding program's credits) reminding viewers to "stay tuned for . . ." was the most obvious example of such flow techniques. Williams also considered the very continuity of programming from evening to the late hours in the night to be a source of continuity itself (television in the United Kingdom was at that time largely limited to the evening).

Today such strategies are even more pervasive: credits whiz by at very high speeds and are miniaturized and pushed to the corner of the screen while previews of upcoming programs continually roll. Advertisements increasingly take on the aesthetics and theme of the programs they are supporting (particularly big events such as movie premieres and sports specials). The networks also remind viewers of the flow of particular evenings with the promotion of themes such as "Must See TV," "Saturday Night Thrillogy," "Monstervision," or the testosterone-laced "movies for guys who like movies."

Benefiting from Williams's thoughts on television and information flow, *Profiling Machines* questions the techniques by which individuals are *continuously* integrated into a larger information economy and technological apparatus. As I discuss at length in chapter 3, a pivotal moment in profiling in the information society is the point at which human tastes, desires, and opinions are actively solicited or accumulated. Since such information must always be diagnosed and cross-referenced with other data (see chapter 4), profiles are also actively constructed through a network of information technologies and databases. Introducing this diagnostic element to Williams's concept of "flow," then, Manuel Castells (1996) characterizes this "networking" logic as an incessant process of modification and analysis. In fostering this networked economy, Castells (1996, 32) notes that

> What characterizes the current technological revolution is not the centrality of knowledge and information, but the application of such knowledge and information to knowledge generation and information processing/communication devices, in a cumulative feedback loop between innovation and uses of innovation.

However, to argue that such networking is in some manner new or unique would be clearly shortsighted. For as James R. Beniger (1986) notes in his historical study of information technologies in the late nineteenth and early twentieth centuries, technological networks began in earnest with the industrial revolution in the mid-eighteenth century. Offering instances of administrative disorganization in economic production, such as poor transportation linkages between the northeastern hub of the United States and the south, Beniger (1986, 219) documents the rise in bureaucratic and administrative control mechanisms (engaging with sociologists such as Max Weber and Anthony Giddens). The innovation of counting machines (punched-card readers) from the likes of

Herman Hollerith (soon to be cofounder of IBM) speaks to the rationalization and management of the population in the form of the census. The organization of efficient transportation and communication "routes" such as canals, railways, and telegraph and telephone lines likewise facilitated increased control over the larger sphere of economic production. More to the point, the growth in research techniques, particularly "feedback technologies" (market research, including Gallup and Nielsen polls), also introduced the views of the population into the information "loop" (Beniger 1986, 376–398).

THE POLITICS OF PROFILING: MAPS AND SIMULATIONS

As economies, information technologies, and production, distribution, and consumption "loops" have become increasingly more pervasive and complex, critical studies of social control and inventory systems have focused on the question of the rights and freedoms of individuals. Although Michel Foucault's work draws on a somewhat distant European past and has a specific historical perspective, his interest in techniques of categorization, surveillance, and social control have been taken up by many contemporary cultural theorists who are perplexed by a culture that has become overdetermined by technological networks. In this regard, Foucault's *Discipline and Punish: The Birth of the Prison* (1977), particularly his architectural discussion of Jeremy Bentham's Panopticon prison, has been the source of much lively debate. Contemporary criticism has interpreted Foucault's work in light of the rise of information technologies and networks in government, the workplace, education, and consumer markets. A central question that pervades much of this work is how we are to understand surveillance across—not necessarily "outside" of—isolated, fixed, and imprisoned spaces as well as wider urban, rural, and geographical spaces.

Modern forms of surveillance, as Christopher Dandeker's *Surveillance, Power, and Modernity: Bureaucracy and Discipline from 1700 to the Present Day* (1989), reminds us, can be traced back to the rise of bureaucratic and legal forms of governance. Dandeker (1989, 37–38) describes the shift in power relations as moving from forms of "supervision" to "bureaucratic surveillance." Such a shift could be understood simply in terms of the directness or immediacy of forms of control and management. The supervisor's morning "Hello," for example, serves as a gentle reminder of the need to arrive at the workplace on time. In a system based on bureaucratic surveillance, conversely, workers simply punch a time card into a clock, removing the need for direct supervision of arrival times. Rules and technologies are therefore established to ensure the worker's compliance with the work schedule and expected level of production.

Steven Nock's *The Costs of Privacy: Surveillance and Reputation in America* (1993) offers a more systemic, or sociological, explanation for the rise of supervisory and bureaucratic forms of surveillance. Nock methodically details the changes in domestic living arrangements in the immediate post–World War II period, finding plenty of evidence to support his contention that children became independent of their parents at increasingly earlier ages. Moreover, children also moved out of their parent's homes in large numbers, greatly increasing the number of single-occupant domiciles in the United States. Nock contends (quite rightly, I believe) that such changes led to a heightened sense of privacy and individualism. Without the family, society needed to institutionalize new social forms of control. For Nock (1993, 5–6), surveillance was the cost that society had to pay for an increased need for privacy. Greater and greater numbers of people were strangers to each other, and their ability to interact with and to trust individuals was compromised. Surveillance, then, filled in for the demise of "reputations," resulting in the establishment of increasingly bureaucratized and institutionalized forms of credentials—credit, education, identification.

Such analyses and histories of surveillance provide much needed perspectives on trends in information systems. However, to respond to more pervasive systems of surveillance—outside the home and the workplace—contemporary theories have increasingly focused on issues of privacy and overt forms of discrimination. There are many differing approaches to surveillance, but the study of "dataveillance" provides a useful point of departure for discussion and analysis. The term *dataveillance* is widely attributed to Roger A. Clarke (1988), a scholar of information systems and technologies. Clarke has studied the computer's contributions to the redefinition of systems of surveillance and defines *dataveillance* as the systematic use of personal data systems to monitor behavior. Clarke's study, entitled "Information Technology and Dataveillance," is one of the most comprehensive attempts at classifying various forms of surveillance. The major distinction that he draws in his study is between personal forms of surveillance (focusing on issues of criminal behavior) and mass surveillance (focusing on issues of social control). Although Clarke recognizes the role played by profiling or computer matching in predicting deviant behavior, he nonetheless fails to acknowledge a potential for discriminatory practices against individuals and communities. For example, the profiling of drug suspects (an instance of personal surveillance, according to Clarke) often leads to the systematic harassment of young men of color in the United States (surely a mass phenomenon).

Mark Poster's *The Mode of Information: Poststructuralism and Social Context* (1990), particularly the chapter on "Foucault and Databases," similarly takes Clarke's term *dataveillance* as a central line of inquiry. Engaging with poststructural theories of language, Poster is, however, more concerned with the database as a new medium than he is with any systemic notion of privacy or discrimination. Speaking more directly to Foucault's work, Poster (1990, 93) discusses surveillance as a "Superpanopticon" that creeps out of the recesses of architectures to the larger topographical terrain. Poster (1990, 91) has also argued that databases are not an invasion of privacy but rather that they constitute a means of "adjusting and readjusting *ad infinitum* the norm of individuality." David Lyon's *The Electronic Eye: The Rise of Surveillance Society* (1994) is similarly influenced by Clarke but questions Poster's evacuation of personhood and agency. By maintaining some sense of an individual as a "self-communicating" entity, Lyon (1994, 52) argues that surveillance works through a series of solicitations and seductions whereby individuals actively "trigger" their own inclusion into systems of surveillance.

Oscar H. Gandy's *The Panopticon Sort: A Political Economy of Personal Information* (1993), perhaps the most detailed work on surveillance from the perspective of computers and dataveillance, engages both the poststructural and political economy traditions. Again focusing on the role of data in government, education, and consumer markets, Gandy argues that the contemporary information system sorts individuals and communities into abstract categories. In such an economy, notions of privacy are replaced by an understanding of the larger political and economic effects of the loss of control over personal information. Gandy's central contribution stems from his insistence that this process of sorting individuals and groups is inherently discriminatory, a belief that is directly discussed in his essay aptly entitled "It's Discrimination, Stupid" (1995). In the essay, Gandy (1995, 42) forwards a notion of "group privacy" based on the fact that surveillance systems work in particular geographies, through the use of zip codes, school districts, and other geographic markers. Gandy's insistence on geographic variables is a welcome corrective to the overemphasis on data and repositories of data in the works of Clarke,

Lyon, and Poster, yet it remains largely underdeveloped and untheorized.

While almost all of the authors discussed above mention profiling or computer matching at one time or another in their works (albeit mostly in passing), few equate such processes with the need for simulations and visual representations in surveillance systems (see chapter 4 for a discussion of the importance of computer mapping programs such as geographical information systems). The process of establishing a category or profile of a potential transgressor of rules (such as a criminal or deviant) must by definition precede the act of transgression itself. Taking the view of dataveillance, this would entail a process of cross-referencing patterns of behavior to establish commonalties among transgressors—a profile. The form that this profile takes (and ultimately where the dataveillance approach ends) is a typographical list or simple printout. For example, in the case of a criminal profile, the list could read "five feet tall, Caucasian, single, passive aggressive, a loner with a history of mental illness"). In the police station, however, the typographical profile is only the beginning of the investigative process. Typographical profiles are almost always followed by visual representations—sometimes a picture but often (as a result of the need to locate possible future sites of transgression) a map.

With these thoughts in mind, consider William Bogard's *The Simulation of Surveillance: Hypercontrol in Telematic Societies* (1996), in which he discusses the processes of profiling and surveillance in relation to simulations. According to Bogard (1996, 34–35), surveillance attempts to "look through" or "around" something, whereas simulations are "projected onto something" (such as screens). The theoretical—and by extension, political—strength of Bogard's work is his rejection of Jean Baudrillard's theory of simulation, which is dominated by questions of sensibility and the collapse of true/false distinctions.[4] Instead, Bogard (1996, 14) turns to the work of Gilles Deleuze, who maintains that simulations or "the virtual" should not be likened to the "actual" but rather to the "possible." Thus, for Deleuze, simulations are always working toward potential situations and goals, producing effects on individuals and groups. Bogard uses the Deleuzian definition of *simulation* to discuss surveillance and profiling as predictive technologies in space. In other words, for Bogard, simulations of surveillance provide maps of potential transgressions in space. Such simulations give us the ability to change spatial arrangements and the behavior of individuals and groups.

To summarize, while all theories of surveillance speak to the shifting social fabric of everyday life, few relate issues of privacy, power, and discrimination to the processes and effects of simulational technological systems. And while concerns over privacy continue to mount, Gandy reminds us that information systems increasingly place individual wants and desires into larger, rationalized, and easily diagnosable profiles (demographics and psychographics). Surveillance in this light cannot be removed from notions of social control or from the potential for certain preplanned effects.

THE DIAGRAM IN ACTION

This book is roughly divided into three sections. Chapters 1 and 2 attempt to provide a theoretical framework for the remainder of the book. Engaging the work of Michel Foucault, Gilles Deleuze, and Felix Guattari, this "diagrammatic" approach attempts to account for both the automation of solicitation technologies and the simulational dimension of demographic mapping. The book invokes the term *diagrammatics* as a particular analytical method in much the same way that linguists and cultural critics such as Roland Barthes, Charles Peirce, and Ferdinand de Saussure invoke *signification*, but diagrammatics generates meaning in the process of *continuously* redefining itself. And while this diagrammatic approach owes much to Foucault's panoptic writings (the panopticon itself—the "all-seeing" institution—being an example of a "diagram"), it does so critically. Chapter 2, for instance, explicitly questions the continued application of Foucault's disciplinary panopticon as a productive model for the *contemporary* study of personal information (demographics and psychographics). At the heart of the matter is Foucault's (and others', including at times Deleuze's) insistence on the larger societal, geographical, and simulational dimensions of the panoptic mode of surveillance. Emphasizing the simulational element of panopticism, Foucault refers to the carceral model as merely a "diagram" of power, indeed one that was never realized by its designer, Jeremy Bentham. Other than this one reference, Foucault does not explicitly return to the question of simulation, surveillance, or the geography of new information technologies. It is consequently Deleuze and Guattari, individually and collaboratively, who push the limits of Foucault's architectural metaphors and who redefine the "diagram" in simulational terms as a process or "modulation" rather than a particular "mold" (Deleuze 1992a, 4). A central metaphor that Deleuze, in particular, mobilizes in support of his diagram is the map, a model (or "machine") of signification that engages in an incessant process of redefinition. This chapter consequently puts the materialist pretensions of Foucault, Deleuze, and Guattari's diagrammatic philosophies to work on the various modes of data accumulation, diagnosis, and simulation in the geodemographic economy.

Chapters 3 and 4 of the book turn to a more schematic approach to the spatial and technological understanding of feedback technologies. Chapter 3 provides a historical perspective on particular technological innovations that originated in the business and government sectors and that have facilitated both the automation and networking of feedback technologies, integrating the consumer's demographic and psychographic data into a production, distribution, and sales "loop." Going beyond purely visual critiques of consumer culture and advertising, this chapter traces the various techniques and technologies of consumer solicitations, beginning with the American census in the late nineteenth century. The key component in this historical study is the means by which such solicitations are automated into computer networks, particularly those connected to other spheres of commercial and governmental decision making and marketing. Drawing on other examples— such as warranty cards and point-of-sale technologies such as rebate or membership (bar-coded) cards—the chapter discusses the manner in which the act of consumption is increasingly defined by the decentralization and routinization of various solicitation techniques and by the production of computerized networks of such transaction-generated information (such as consumer databases).

Building on this topographic and networked understanding of consumption, chapter 4 then moves to a discussion of how geodemographic mapping software forecasts or simulates spatial patterns of consumer markets (among a host of other variables relating to production, distribution, and sales). The chapter begins with a basic discussion of the various categories of personal information and moves on to explicate the spatial implications of profiling. The process by which psychographic categories are created subsequently sheds light on the attempt to discriminate individuals by their particular lifestyles—a culmination of many cross-referenced variables. Such categories form the basis or rather the "target" for most if not all contemporary marketing campaigns, services, and products. Yet without geodemographic information, in particular, the diagnosis and ultimately the use of such profiles would be greatly limited. This chapter therefore highlights the means by which such lifestyle-defined, psychographic profiles are cross-referenced with geographical sources of information (such as zip codes or school and electoral districts), continuously producing computer-generated maps of probable consumer markets.

Chapters 5 and 6 of the book focus on a pair of case studies—a marketing event in the Canadian Arctic (Molson's "Polar Beach Party") and the use of "cookies" to collect personal information from Web users. The Polar Beach Party described in chapter 5 is a marketing event that interrupts the predictable flow of commercial iconography in everyday life. It highlights the tension between the wealthy event attendees from the United States and southern Canada and the demographically authentic, though psychographically insignificant, indigenous peoples of the Canadian Arctic. Chapter 6 takes the hypertextual environment of the Web as its focus. Building on the historical trajectory of automated and networked feedback outlined in chapter 2, this chapter first discusses the manner in which particular technologies (such as spiders, robots, intelligent agents, and cookies) format the hypertextual spaces of the Web in a way that automates the process of demographic solicitation. With these new technologies, a mere "browse" of a particular Web site automates the transfer of certain demographic information (such as address, length of visit, and links followed) from the user to the producer and thereby further redefines the act and definition of "consumption" and the possibilities of discriminatory practices. It is also noted that the tracking and surveillance capabilities of cookies have spawned a series of like-minded strategies by computer and Internet industries.

Feedback technologies are not all-pervasive or Orwellian in nature, however, and the book concludes (in chapter 7) with an attempt to politicize the topographical dimension of the "habitual" (as articulated in the works of Pierre Bourdieu and Michel de Certeau). Responses to profiling technologies, as a whole, must take into consideration the more pervasive "default culture"—the systematic incorporation of technological choices in absence of consumer responses. These default settings inevitably entrench economic and political interests (consider, for example, the bundling of Microsoft's Web browser). A critical understanding of the discriminatory power of contemporary, "cybernetic capitalism" (Robins & Webster 1988) is therefore best served by questioning the everyday, spatialized routines that increasingly intersect with networked consumer and governmental databases, computerized maps, and mass-mediated images of the landscapes that we—and so-called others—inhabit.

2

As consumers make purchases, request catalogues, return goods for servicing and repair, or simply browse for desirable commodities and services, their transactions are duly noted, stored, cross-referenced, and often tracked or mapped. This process is ubiquitous and has broad implications for the study of techniques of social control, consumerism, market rationalization, and risk management. For the many critics of consumer surveillance, the theoretical impact of Michel Foucault's (1977) analysis of Jeremy Bentham's seventeenth-century architectural plans for an all-seeing, or panoptic, prison cannot be overstated. Although most critics have attempted to analyze panoptic surveillance from contemporary technological perspectives, this chapter argues that

A DIAGRAM OF PANOPTIC SURVEILLANCE

the development of a theory of panoptic surveillance has been limited by literal readings of Foucault's panoptic prison that are simply critiques of carceral enclosures.

Contemporary interpretations of the panoptic model typically offer one or more of the following three arguments. The first and perhaps the most broadly articulated critique focuses on the shifting architectural and categorical qualities of surveillance, moving from the carceral enclosure of the prison to the consumer database. In attempting to extend the logic of Bentham's Panopticon to contemporary definitions of information, this "dataveillance" critique—first articulated in the expansive scholarship of Roger A.

Clarke[1] but also compellingly revised and adapted in some of the most influential work in contemporary "surveillance studies" (Gandy 1993; Lyon 1994, 2001)—discusses the discriminatory social implications of panopticism, often to expand debates over personal privacy.

By comparison, a second and growing group of scholars has argued that the disciplinary effect of panopticism is not automatic and that contemporary information theory needs to account for a more networked and transparent kind of surveillance. These authors share the view that the transparency of institutional solicitations for information prevents individuals from being easily coerced, forced, or otherwise disciplined into giving up personal information. Rather, they argue that consumers consciously offer their personal information in exchange for a perceived personal benefit (whether a "prize," a rebate, or an exclusive service). Thus, regardless of the enticement, Reg Whitaker (1999, 141) argues, "The Panopticon rewards participation." And while this "enticement" model helps to qualify the process of surveillance as ultimately an act of solicitation and exchange, it also downplays the degree to which such "requests" for personal information are altogether automated (for example, as the Web and browsers initially worked)[2] or realistically provide consumers with viable options to decline the offer (to opt out).

A third group of scholars, many inspired by Tim Mathiesen's (1997) critique of Foucault (1977), has similarly problematized the disciplinary effect of panoptic surveillance. These scholars (Fiske 1993; Bauman 1988; Levin 1997) argue that unlike Foucault's panoptic arrangement of prisoners encircled around a central guard tower, contemporary media technologies are more aptly defined by a *synoptic* relationship where the many now watch the few. John Fiske (1993, 85), for instance, points to the football stadium

as a "reverse panopticon," where the power to individuate, segment, and control gives way to fan power, knowledge, and pleasure (especially when mediated through the multiple angles of
television cameras). The synoptic argument, however, assumes that
panopticism derives from corporeal surveillance—in other words,
that the one literally *watches* the many. However, in the panoptic
prison, disciplinary power does not reside in the "watcher" or
central prison guard; it stems from the architectural arrangement of
light that *suggests* panoptic surveillance to the prisoners. Thus, as a
media critique, the synoptic model is seemingly biased toward
spectatorship. Moreover, as a critique of Foucault's work, it largely
fails to note how synopticism and panopticism potentially work in
concert.

These three variations of panoptic criticism are more nuanced and
often overlapping in their contributions than initially described
here. Nevertheless, as I soon show in greater detail, the categorization of such critiques is helpful in expanding the theoretical
debate over the relevance and applicability of Foucault's panoptic
model, particularly in an increasingly complex economy of personal information. Moreover, such critiques have distinct implications for claims made about the dubious social effects of panoptic
surveillance. The enticement and synoptic critiques, for example,
can lead to a relatively unfettered notion of consumer agency
and choice where private information is consciously bartered and
exchanged for a perceived benefit. By contrast, dataveillance
arguments often result in questions about the technological ability
to guarantee privacy. Ultimately, chapter 7 argues that all three
critiques of panoptic surveillance are limited by their heuristic
points of departure—the technology or architecture of panopticism (dataveillance), the solicitation and exchange of personal
information (enticement), and the reverse panopticon where the
many watch the few (synoptic model).

With the help of Foucault and his "interlocutor" Gilles Deleuze and collaborator Felix Guattari, chapter 7 conversely theorizes panoptic surveillance as a process that quantifies and qualifies the behaviors of consumers (or other sales, inventory, or distribution data) and also the efficiency of the panoptic process itself. Such an overarching theory of surveillance (or even an appreciation of the specific dynamics of panopticism, such as data accumulation or storage) cannot privilege any one step in the process of panoptic surveillance by focusing exclusively on questions such as "How is personal information solicited?" or "How and where are personal information and other forms of consumer data stored (in databases or networked systems)?" Consequently, in explicating the *diagrammatic* characteristics of panoptic surveillance, this chapter attempts to account for how consumers and their personal data become *continuously* integrated into the collecting, storing, and cross-referencing of a multitude of consumer market data (inventory, distribution, and sales).

PANOPTICS, CONFESSIONS, AND SOLICITATIONS

The widespread tendency to focus on specific characteristics of the panopticon is hardly surprising given Michel Foucault's often contradictory, vague, and sometimes brief passages. As a whole, *Discipline and Punish: The Birth of the Prison* (1977) is seemingly marked by a number of contradictions, the most obvious being an instance of violent closure, literally confinement, bumping up against the poststructuralist aversion to binary systems or Cartesian models. Following a philosophical tradition overdetermined by questions of vision and light (cf. Jay 1993), David Michael Levin (1997, 404) also argues that the thesis of self-discipline and governance in Foucault's carceral vision machine is dependent on the very object of critique—the hegemony of light, vision, and the gaze. Thus, because prisoners are not able to view the guard in the panopticon's centrally located tower, they must assume an all-seeing gaze as marked and yet masked, at once visible and invisible. Foucault's thesis follows that since prisoners must therefore assume that at any time they could be under the watchful eye of the guard in the tower, they begin to self-discipline their behavior.

Suggesting a link to contemporary forms of data storage, however, Foucault (1977, 198) reminds us that the panopticon is a system of both light and language—a system of optic surveillance that is predicated on and reinforced by the documentation and distribution of personal information. Gilles Deleuze (1986, 18) likewise notes the productive tension in Foucault's work between the use of the visible and expressible: "language coagulates around a corpus only in order to facilitate the distribution or dispersion of statements and to stand as the rule for a 'family' that is naturally dispersed." Thus, in addition to providing a visual element of power and of self-imposed discipline that is driven by an inability to see agents of authority, the panopticon provides a simple classificatory architecture, an archive in which individuals or bodies are separated and classified with the assistance of files.

In addition to questions of light and language, Foucault's writings also offer a seemingly ambiguous theory of surveillance, institutions, and space. Although he seemed almost caught off guard by such criticisms in a published interview in *Power/Knowledge: Selected Interviews and Other Writings, 1972–1977* (1980), Foucault's attachment to enclosed spaces in other works, such as *Madness and Civilization: A History of Insanity in the Age of Reason* (1965) and *The Birth of the Clinic: An Archaeology of Medical Perception* (1973), are explicitly described as "a *generalizable* model of functioning: a way of defining power relations in terms of everyday life" (1977, 205) (my emphasis). Nevertheless, Foucault's one attempt to give a geographical representation of panopticism, at the outset of *Discipline and Punish* (1977, 196), is a decidedly indexical or archival form of surveillance:

> At the beginning of the "lock up," the role of each of the inhabitants present in the town is laid down, one by one; this document bears "the name, age, sex of everyone, notwithstanding his condition": a copy is sent to the intendant of the quarter, another to the office of the town hall, another to enable the syndic to make his daily roll call. Everything that may be observed during the course of the visits—deaths, illnesses, complaints, irregularities—is noted down and transmitted to the intendants and magistrates.

In addition to lingering architectural and spatial questions, a pivotal dimension of Foucault's powerful discriminatory apparatus, particularly for contemporary studies of consumer surveillance, is the exposition of data accumulation—the means by which information is "solicited" from individuals. Foucault's panoptic architecture therefore remains formidably closed and static, for prisoners are fixed in their respective cells with no possibility of movement or escape from the potential gaze of the central tower. In fact, the panopticon's prisoners, as surveyed data-subjects, are categorized and segmented before they are "solicited," albeit quite forcefully, for personal information (such as behavior). The prison's architecture—the spatial segmentation of bodies within a system of light—facilitates that accumulation of information. Then again, in keeping with his previous thoughts on broader topographical questions, Foucault maintains that he is more interested in the general deployment of a system of power that calls on individuals to self-discipline their own behavior than he is with the specifics of architecture. Thus, Foucault's (1977, 220, 206) invocation of an ongoing system of "continuous registration, perpetual assessment and classification" that increases its efficiency through "increasing its own points of contact" raises the question of how we might conceptualize the multiple interactions between *mobile* subjects and geographically dispersed technologies of surveillance.

In particular, the overtly fixed nature of confinement and discipline in the panoptic prison tends to erase the technological nuances of data accumulation—the significance of repetition, habit, corporeal movement, and the flow of everyday life. Foucault later suggests in the *History of Sexuality: An Introduction* (1978, 61) that behavior is also modified when it is placed into language, whereby the confession of a secret produces a paradoxically unadulterated "truth." And while Foucault (1978, 60) again focuses on the practice of confessions in institutionalized religion, he is quick to extend this logic into the realm of the topographical, where

> the obligation to confess is now relayed through so many points, is so deeply ingrained in us, that we no longer perceive it as the effect of a power that constrains us.

Typically, theorists of consumer surveillance have viewed Foucault's qualifications and generalizations of panoptic surveillance as inconsistencies and limitations. All too often, such critiques have focused on the prison at the expense of panopticism or the technology as opposed to the technique. This chapter, however, argues that the panoptic process, manifest in consumer-surveillance technologies, is driven by a panoptic "generality," characterized herein as a blueprint or carceral "diagram." For as Foucault (1977, 205) reminds us, the panoptic "dream building" was but a "*diagram* of a mechanism of power reduced to its ideal form; its functioning, abstracted from any obstacle, resistance, or friction, must be represented as a pure architectural and optical system: it is in fact a political technology that may and must be detached from any specific use" (emphasis added).

Dataveillance was first defined by privacy expert Roger A. Clarke (1988, 499) as "the systemic use of personal data systems in the investigation or monitoring of one or more persons." From the outset, then, Clarke focused on how new information and communication technologies extend the power of the observers to monitor the actions of individuals and communities. The term *dataveillance*, however, also suggests that the act of surveillance is enabled and perhaps even enhanced through the close monitoring of information produced by consumer interactions and exchanges (credit-card purchases, ATM withdrawals, and so on). In "Information Technology and Dataveillance" (1988), Clarke thus set out to distinguish dataveillance from forms of mass and personal surveillance by concentrating on the use of computerized storage and networking technologies—in short, by discussing the various techniques of computerized monitoring. Dataveillance, moreover, entails decentralizing the panoptic mode of surveillance, calling into question the production of risk-management tools—computer-matching or -profiling techniques that attempt to attribute general characteristics to individuals. When applied to the implications of cross-referencing multiple types of personal information, Clarke's approach inevitably leads to concern over the failures of such systems—that is, their production of ill-fitting profiles that fail to match the actual likes, dislikes, and behaviors of an individual.

Although Clarke's technological discussion of contemporary dataveillance clearly expands panopticism into the realm of decentralized computer databases and their accompanying profiling and predictive technologies, he begins his critique with an already surveyed, or initially classified, subject. In other words, Clarke does not question how, when, and where information is collected on individuals. As Foucault suggests, though, panoptic surveillance relies as much on the decentralization of information processing (via decenteralized and networked databases) as it does on geographically dispersed, "feedback technologies" that can pinpoint and track the topography of consumer interactions.

Recent updates of the dataveillance literature, particularly by David Lyon, have attempted to address certain gaps in Clarke's initial work. Lyon, for instance, qualifies the moment at which information is collected on individuals, arguing that consumers often "trigger" their own surveillance. Lyon's most recent book, *Surveillance Society: Monitoring Everyday Life* (2001), also warns that contemporary surveillance technologies are enabled by "leaky containers." The metaphor is a compelling one, suggesting the power of networked technologies and the ultimate futility of database security and consumer privacy. However, while the term *container* suggests an enclosure such as a database, Lyon's sole example discusses the visual collection (and not storage per se) of personal information—video surveillance of workplace behavior. Thus, Lyon's "leaky container" metaphor points to the convergence of technological systems and subsequent ubiquity of surveillance techniques and technologies in society.

We might therefore consider how the collection of personal information is also "bundled" to the storage and cross-referencing of other data. Bundling is used to highlight the interface between the collection, storage, and cross-referencing of consumer data and other forms of sales, inventory, and distribution data (what are often called "just-in-time" delivery systems). One such "interface"—the moment at which individuals are solicited for personal information—is the prime focus of "enticement" theories of consumer surveillance. Such arguments tend to focus on the political or "disciplinary" consequences of Foucault's work, often asking whether we can conceive of consumers as conscious or willing "participants" in their own surveillance. A number of techniques are used to solicit information from users. Some are relatively transparent and carry little disciplinary implications for nonparticipation—being asked to fill out a survey in a shopping mall, for instance. Computer-aided solicitations, by comparison, tend to be much less forgiving or exclusively rewarding. They subtly integrate both rewards *and* punishments. Shoppers, for example, who decline or merely neglect to sign up for bar-coded discount cards end up paying a significantly higher price for an increasing array of products. Thus, even if consumers know that information is being collected on them, their choices are either "participation" or the default "punishment" of a higher price. Simon Davies (1998, 144) aptly refers to this incentive to "opt in" as the "illusion of voluntariness."

The assumption that one can voluntarily opt in or out of data-collection techniques is not valid for some feedback technologies. ATM machines, portions of the Web, and credit-card transactions, for instance, *automatically* collect personal information from users. Thus, just as the panopticon automates the process of how prisoners self-discipline their own behavior, these technologies likewise automate the collection of transaction-generated information and the subsequent "choice" to divulge personal information. Ultimately, the conclusions of the enticement argument are somewhat clouded by a coercive definition of panoptic surveillance. Such extensions of Foucault's work often lend themselves to equally rigid terms, despite being defined as open, optional, and transparent. A more subtle definition of feedback technologies requires a rethinking of the nature of consumer exchanges and questions the degree to which the production and collection of transaction-generated information become inseparable and continuous parts of the act of consumption—whether defined as purchasing, booking, browsing, or requesting information about products or services.

The question of technological control, discussed by both entice-ment and dataveillance scholars, is by contrast largely bypassed in Tim Mathiesen's (1997) theory of "synopticism." Although some might be inclined to see his inverted critique of panoptic surveil-lance as a wholesale rejection of Foucault's disciplinary thesis, Mathiesen (1997, 219) notes that the "synopticon" works in "par-allel to the panoptical process." Perhaps as a way to generalize Foucault's interest in social forms of control, Mathiesen points to the mass media as a pivotal space where the many watch the select few opinion leaders and celebrities. Unlike Foucault's panopticon, the automatic modification of behavior in the synopticon is much less obvious. Mathiesen (1997, 230) argues that social control is exerted by media messages "disciplining our *consciousness*." And although television and its "few" are generally agreed to possess varying degrees of power to cultivate the terms of political, eco-nomic, and social debate and consciousness, this synoptic pro-cess is also greatly enhanced through more traditional panoptic techniques—a parallel process that Mathiesen recognizes but does not develop.

Synoptic viewing of television programming is increasingly facili-tated by a panoptic process integrated into the medium of tele-vision and by extension the act of watching television. Recent digital TV technology, for example, has begun to incorporate the collection of personal information within the act of viewing and recording programming. Initially marketed as a stand-alone "per-sonal" or "digital" video recorder (DVR), TiVo is now also a recording service that has been incorporated into cable receivers by major U.S. digital cable (AT&T Broadband) and satellite television (DirecTV) providers. Moreover, television scholar William Boddy (1999) notes that

One feature of the personal video recorder of enormous appeal to networks and advertisers is its ability to continuously track users' viewing preferences, offering sponsors and broadcasters the long-sought ability to deliver tailored commercials to individually targeted consumers. General Motors, for example, has partnered with TiVo to allow the replacement of a GM broadcast advertisement with another commercial previously downloaded on the household's PVR, one tailored to the consumer's specific viewing habits and demographic profile.

The pivotal shift that TiVo adds to the synoptic act of television viewing is the recommendation-customization function. According to the corporation, TiVo "uses Anonymous Viewing Information to develop inferences that people who watch show X are likely to watch show Y" (TiVo 2001, 16). Based on this process of viewer profiling, TiVo recommends "like-minded" programming. In other words, if a viewer watches *Monty Python*, TiVo would most likely recommend John Cleese's *Fawlty Towers*. Or if a viewer routinely watches reruns of *Cheers*, TiVo would likely recommend the spinoff, *Frasier*. In addition to serving as a recommender system, the viewing data that TiVo collects also serves to link specific advertisements to a subset of consumers who have previously demonstrated through their viewing habits an affiliation with the product or service. The panoptic power of TiVo thus raises questions far beyond those posed by the synoptic relationship between the viewer and the viewed, whose claims to privacy and "resistive readings" are constantly debated. In short, TiVo reminds us that the select few that we watch (synoptically) are becoming even more select (via a panoptic process)—that viewers are getting exceptionally familiar, "more of the same" programming.

This subtle form of limiting access to *difference* does not rely on individualized forms of identification—a process that individual privacy advocates continue to question. TiVo, in fact, goes out of its way to emphasize that all information collected on viewers is anonymous. Panopticism, as such, does not "multiply the individual" (Poster 1990, 97) as much as it uses the collection of personal information to discriminate individuals into previously categorized consumer lifestyle groups or "profiles." The always already discriminated and profiled data subject thus highlights the need to theorize the reproduction of panoptic surveillance—that is, the means by which the collection, storage, and cross-referencing of personal information continuously inform each other. This cybernetic aspect of panoptic surveillance requires a rethinking—and redrawing—of the panoptic diagram.

A MODULATING THEORY OF SURVEILLANCE

The term *diagrammatics* has been evoked by a number of individuals associated with the philosophy of art, logic, and language. Apart from the previously quoted passage from *Discipline and Punish* (1977), Foucault himself makes no other specific references to "diagrams," a diagrammatic method, or on a more general level, contemporary information and communication technologies. An explicitly diagrammatic approach has therefore been largely conferred onto Foucault's works by Gilles Deleuze. John Marks (1994, 98) rightly argues that Deleuze's primary purpose in consistently returning to the concept of the diagram was to push the limits of Foucault's "spatial metaphors." Hence, in an attempt to capture the tension between these two authors, D. N. Rodowick (1990, 17) has argued that perhaps

> The most succinct way of defining the diagram is to call it a map of power—diagrammatics is the cartography of strategies of power. As such, the diagram produces a historical image of how strategies of power attempt to replicate

themselves in forms of surveillance, documentation, and expression on one hand, and in the spatial organization of collective life on the other.

The death of Gilles Deleuze in 1995 (over a decade after Foucault's passing in 1984) heightened the mythical narratives surrounding the two influential philosophers. Their numerous published exchanges, interviews, collaborations, and references to each other's work may have even discouraged any sustained critical discussion of the productive differences between the two authors. In other words, their exchanges were distinctly complementary and collegial in tone, emphasizing, for example, a shared commitment to conceptualizing "tools" or methodologies for political life (Deleuze & Foucault 1972). In the preface to Deleuze and Guattari's *Anti-Oedipus: Capitalism and Schizophrenia* (1983, xii), Foucault insists that "Informed by the seemingly abstract notions of multiplicities, flows, arrangements, and connections, [Deleuze and Guattari's work] yields answers to concrete questions." Deleuze (1992b, 165), likewise, characterizes Foucault's work as engaging in the study of "precise archives" and employing "extremely new historical methods."

With the publication of the essay "Postscript on Societies of Control" (1992a) and the book *Foucault* (1986), Deleuze began to question and relate panoptic forms of surveillance and contemporary information economies. This was a shift from architectural and optical modes of surveillance to the integration of dispersed sites of information solicitation within simulational feedback loops. Deleuze (1992a, 4) questions the applicability of spaces of enclosure with direct reference to his colleague Foucault, arguing that disciplinary apparatuses (panopticon prisons, hospitals, and factories) function as mere "Enclosures" or "molds, distinct castings," whereas throughout geographic spaces "controls are a modulation." For Deleuze, the concept of "modulation" emphasizes the manner in which relations of power are themselves reproduced in and through technological networks. Francisco Varela, likewise, compares "allopoietic" machines (which produce "something other than themselves" in the process of constituting "their own organization and limits") to the modulating "autopoietic machines," which, conversely, "undertake ... the replacement of their components" to "continually compensate for the external perturbations to which they are exposed" (Guattari 1995: 39).

Thus, in attempting to offer a corrective to the Foucaultian panopticon, Gilles Deleuze offers the concept of "rhizomatic" or nomadic movement. Deleuze posits his contemporary rhizomatic diagram as existing in a perpetual state between the architectural processes of drawing and building; and in so doing he attempts to avoid the primacy of the visual or fixed architectural structure (enclosure). Hence, in Deleuze's (1986, 35, 44) own words,

> The diagram is no longer an auditory or visual archive but a map, a cartography that is coextensive with the whole social field. [Furthermore, the] ... diagram is a map, or rather several superimposed maps. And from one diagram to the next, new maps are drawn. Thus, there is no diagram that does not also include, besides the points which it connects up, certain relatively free or unbound points, points of creativity, change and resistance, and it is perhaps with these that we ought to begin in order to understand the whole picture.

This cybernetic and topographical dimension of both surveillance and simulation—originally characterized by its complex "pattern of computation" in the act of "forecasting the future" (Wiener 1948, 13)—has been largely overlooked in contemporary Foucaultian or panoptic studies of personal information, consumer data, and information technologies. Taking a diagrammatic approach to panoptic surveillance conversely requires us to conceptualize the manner in which modes of data accumulation, storage, and processing are networked in an increasingly dispersed and automated infoscape.

Perhaps mindful of criticizing his deceased colleague, Deleuze at once juxtaposes and links the disciplinary logic of Foucault's panopticon from its architectural "molds" to a theory of power based on "modulations." Thus, in a telling passage from his essay "What Is a Dispositif?" Deleuze (1992b, 164) walks a fine line between Foucault's panopticon (merely describing "the history of what we gradually cease to be") and a much more schematic difference between "closed disciplines" and systems of "overt and continuous control." Implicitly siding with Marxists such as Henri Lefebrve, who believed that Foucault failed to theorize the "collective subject" (Soja 1996, 146), Deleuze (1995, 179–180) also juxtaposes the individualistic element of disciplinary society with that of societies of control:

> Disciplinary societies have two poles: signatures standing for *individuals*, and numbers or places in a register standing for their position in a *mass.* . . . In control societies, on the other hand, the key thing is no longer a signature or number but a code.

Departing from molds or architectures of confinement that segment, categorize, and discipline individual "deviants," Deleuze's thoughts on the "diagram" attempt to account for the systemic modulations of populations by technological machines and information flows. However, unlike Levin's (1997, 446) synoptic assertion that Foucault's "debilitating blindspot" was an absence of "different contemporary gazes, multiplied and strengthened by our visual technologies" such as television, Deleuze's (1995, 178) "diagrammatic" model emphasizes the simulational aspect of technologies that form "a system of varying geometry whose language is digital." Thus, for Deleuze, the diagram provides a conceptual model for encoding, distributing, and deploying information flows from decentralized apparatuses.

In an attempt to explicate the artistic, corporeal, and rhythmic dimensions of simulation, Deleuze initially appropriates the notion of a "diagram" from Francis Bacon (as discussed in his thoughts on the process of painting). Deleuze was captivated by Bacon's self-described moment of "subversion" where a painter's brush creates a chaotic moment on the surface of the canvas. According to Ronald Bogue (1991, 120), Bacon dubbed such "limited catastrophes" a "diagram." Expanding the discussion to the movement of painting, Deleuze, however, maintains that such diagrams are also characterized by the potential for corporeal rhythm (120). In this respect, Deleuze relates his belief in the continuity and circularity of thought-action—or language-speech—to the realm of production and representation. Hence, before the artist's brush touches the canvas, the painter's actions and motions are *always* within the painting. In Deleuze's (1993, 193) words,

> There is thus preparatory work that fully belongs to painting. This preparatory work may take the form of sketches, but not necessarily, and even sketches do not replace it.... This preparatory work is invisible and silent, but nevertheless very intense.

Although Gilles Deleuze defines diagrammatic production as a corporeal and simulational process, Felix Guattari's definition stems from a distinctly polemical critique of the celebrated semiotic theories of American philosopher Charles Peirce. Guattari specifically challenges Peirce's inclusion of diagrams as icons, drawing a distinction between signifying and asignifying semiotics. For Peirce, a diagram is a representational icon, whereas for Guattari, "the image is both more and less than the diagram: an image reproduces certain things that a diagram does not, while a diagram captures better than an image functional articulations" (Genosko 1996, 17). Guattari's (1977, 95) notion of a diagram is thus often described as a sign machine or blueprint rather than a chain of signifiers. Putting this diagram or sign machine to work thus requires the

> operationalization of signs, this work of diagrammatization ... [becoming] the necessary condition for the deterritorializing mutations that affect the fluxes of reality; no longer is there representation, but simulation, preproduction, or what one might call "transduction."

In addition to the sign or signifier, Guattari also uses the example of the index to define an a-signifying semiotics, typified by the diagram. Guattari argues that in Peirce's schema indexes function as territorial signifiers, pointing to fixed spaces and phenomena (as does, for example, a road map). However, according to Guattari, diagrams also "incorporate certain habits involved in the *creation* of graphic abstractions. . . . they also have the indexical feature of pointing "There!" (Genosko 1996, 18). For both Deleuze and Guattari, this ongoing *production* of relationships and associations is characterized by a certain level of abstraction and is also grounded in a functional, spatial politics—one that attempts to locate and map the circulation of information, data, power, and control. Explaining the shared approach, Guattari (in Deleuze 1995, 21–22) offers a wonderfully succinct comment:

> We're strict functionalists: what we're interested in is how something works, functions—finding the machine. But the signifier is still stuck in the question "What does it mean?"

With the emergence of increasingly more complex and "inhabited" virtual spaces, transjurisdictional territories, and intranets (computerized informational networks), archives of information are now characterized by their multiple sites, processes, and techniques of input, storage, and retrieval. In such a flux of affairs, Deleuze and Guattari rightly focus on the function of territorializing "machines," mapping the real-time machinations of a data *dispositif*. Engaging the concept of the diagram from Bacon, Peirce, and Foucault, Deleuze and Guattari introduce the possibility of tracing or sketching the continuity between light and language. In the realm of contemporary infomatics, the diagram therefore allows us to trace the everyday data economy in which habits, routines, rhythms, and flows are digitized, coded, and diagnosed for the purposes of control. An impressive number of solicitations have for the large part been automated within other areas of cultural practice—most notably consumption. Solicitations of personal information are, in other words, not so much expressed or articulated as much as they are automated and networked into other "duties." Foucault's contributions to this diagrammatic approach to the information economy are in this regard quite clear. In large part, the diagrammatic power of the panopticon lies in its claims to continuity and automation—that is, its ability to function without the need for direct supervision and intervention (cf. Dandeker 1989). In the information economy, such automated systems attempt to continuously collect information on individual behavior (what Foucault dubbed "confessions" with respect to organized religion) to such an extent that individuals regard such solicitations as integral exchanges in everyday life.

Reworking Foucault's panoptic "generality" in light of contemporary, digitized technologies of control, Deleuze characterizes diagrammatics as a simulational process in the making. By focusing on the importance of Bacon's "chaotic" moment (the coming to the fore of a set of loosely preplanned ideas, sketches, and representations), Deleuze explicates the already constituted field of expression and representation (or discriminated and segmented consumers) and also the inherent difficulty in predicting effects (or the wants and desires of consumers). To Foucault's notion of continuity and automation, Deleuze thus adds the circularity or cybernetic dimension to diagrammatics—the manner in which the signifieds and the process of signification are continuously reconstituted by each other. Within the context of corporeal movement and moving away from Foucault's confined body, Deleuze also subtly questions the significance of such cybernetic loops for the everyday rhythms and routines of corporeal movement. Within the context of consumer routines, however, Deleuze's point offers distinct implications for the "interaction" between mobile subjects and sites of demographic and psychographic solicitation. As such, Deleuze again moves toward a more expansive topographical view of exchange whereupon power implicates—and is implicated by—particular places, spaces, and technologies.

Lastly, Guattari's critique of Charles Peirce's semiotics imbues diagrammatics with distinctly diagnostic and machinic qualities. Guattari's frustration with semiotic debates over signs, signifiers, and symbols leads him to critique the innocence with which the processes of signification has abstracted itself from the reproduction of social symbols and the practice, art, and spaces of signification and representation itself. Signification in this diagrammatic sense subsequently incorporates a decidedly economic and machinic element, calling into question the traces of past, present, and future techniques and technologies of rationalization.

INTRANSIGENT FAMILIARITY

As a predictive technique, then, the panoptic diagram calls on an all too familiar aggregated past to subtly limit access to different futures. The removal of uncertainty and by extension the need to make conscious decisions are replaced by an uncannily familiar world of images, goods, and services. Such is the case with digital

television and a host of techniques on the Web, where programming and content are sometimes automatically filtered to reflect past viewing choices. As was shown in the TiVo example, such a networked view of the personal information economy takes us beyond the problematics associated with systems of personal identification or, for that matter, techniques of individuation (in a prison cell or a computer database).

That consumer surveillance often ends up exposing our private lives (such as transactions and demographics) to the world is hardly surprising given the porous state of computer security and privacy laws. Its diagrammatic characteristics also call into question the increasingly intransigent (or disciplinary) technique of making aggregated past consumer behavior (consumer profiles) an instrumental blueprint for possible future consumer products and services or indeed for the very functioning of digital media. A TiVo receiver/recorder, for example, fails to function if it is disconnected (via a phone line) from the TiVo corporation's main office.

The diagrammatic view of panoptic surveillance consequently argues that subjects are not simply surveyed, monitored, or solicited for the purposes of automating a self-medicating acquiescence to social norms and rules (as some Foucaultian scholars might argue). In the panoptic diagram, consumers are not exclusively disciplined: they are both *rewarded* with a preset familiar world of images and commodities and *punished* by having to work at finding different and unfamiliar commodities if they attempt to opt out. The panoptic diagram, in other words, disciplines consumers only if they actively seek out the unfamiliar, the different, the previously unseen, purchased, or browsed. The need to dissuade such transgressive behavior through rewards and punishments is a technological requirement for diagrammatic "just-in-time" systems, where changes in any one aspect of consumer demand, sales, consumption, distribution, and production can drastically effect the whole system.

Thus, as we watch and monitor others and are ourselves monitored, our likes and dislikes are fed back to us, producing a familiar media and consumer environment. We are continuously solicited either with a "more of the same" product or with more inquiries meant to be cross-referenced to monitor new trends and changes in taste or simply to refine the effectiveness and precision of the diagrammatic process itself. As a consequence, we may soon find it compellingly easy and convenient to consume "more of the same" and increasingly more difficult to find something different.

3

As the mediated world becomes increasingly cluttered with commercial appeals, corporate America has responded with a wholesale downsizing of jingles, slogans, and logos. Where there was once Kentucky Fried Chicken, there is now only KFC. Where *General Hospital* and *The Young and the Restless* once graced our screens, there is now simply *GH* and *Y&R*. Similarly, from the increasingly pervasive sphere of advertising, we now find logos, trademarks, and miniaturized symbols accompanying the promotional mantra of such disparate entities as Nike ("Just do it"), Pepsi ("Get free stuff"), the nation-state of Canada ("True north strong and free"), or "the artist formerly known as Prince" ("Party like it's 1999"). Today, however, a select group of corporations (largely blue-chip

CONSUMPTION IN THE NETWORK AGE: SOLICITATION, AUTOMATION, AND NETWORKING

stalwarts such as Coca-Cola, Anheuser-Busch, and McDonald's) have bought so much space in various media—on football pitches, on the ice in ice hockey rinks, on Tiger Woods's T-shirts, or at the eye level of our daily commuter routes—that they have effectively become a natural element of the landscape itself. Although the strategic placement of such condensed trademarks is a relatively recent phenomenon, other marketing techniques have for over a century attempted to locate, interact with, and capitalize on the habits and routines of *probable* consumers of *particular* products.

In their pursuit of demographic and psychographic information about relationships among producers, retailers, and consumers, advertisers and market researchers have condensed complex economic concepts into catchy buzzwords. An article in the *Journal of Advertising Research*, for instance, discusses the economic repercussions of the industrywide growth in "linkage advertising" in which particular images, symbols, or words become distinct messages that also provide consumers with complementary coupons, promotional contests, and 1–800 telephone numbers. The article notes that "two-thirds of all advertising in the United States, Canada, the United Kingdom, and other developed nations includes one or more ways for viewers, listeners, or readers to ... request additional information on the product/service being promoted" (Woodside 1994, 22–32).

In his comments on the increasing importance of customer feedback on services and products, Rob Jackson (1993, 25) has argued that contemporary marketing techniques and strategies should implement an overall "out-in philosophy" based on a system of "in-bound production." The active search and diagnosis of consumer and customer desires "out there" have been driven in part by obvious shifts in demographics, tastes, and trends and in part by a rethinking of the nature of the consumer market itself, which seems to mark a shift in contemporary marketing culture. With increased competition, market deregulation, and increased global trade, an advertising approach that targets its strategies and techniques to a single mass market is now viewed as increasingly costly and ineffective in a world defined by segmented markets. Building on a concept of the mass market that has played a pivotal role in the history of marketing and sales, market researchers have repositioned and redefined the concept within a production, distribution, and sales loop that seemingly incorporates the desires of the individual consumer. For instance, Stanley Davis (1987) coined the phrase *mass customization* to explain "the use of flexible processes and organizational structures to produce varied and often individually customized products and services at the price of standardized, mass produced alternatives" (Hart 1996, 13).

Christopher Hart (1996, 10) similarly argues that a comprehensive marketing strategy that builds on advertising must address the notion of "customer sacrifice"—"the gap between the ideal product-and-service benefits desired by customers and what they actually are able to purchase." That there exists an "ideal" product or service would, however, presuppose an objective set of consumer desires, abstracted from the messages and values cultivated by the advertising industry. Davis's notion of mass customization likewise suggests an ability to customize unique products for individual consumers—that is, to service markets of one.

Both assumptions, however, incorrectly assume that consumer feedback is consciously and willingly offered by consumers, consists of unadulterated opinions on products and services, and directly informs the production of commodities. In an age of networked computers, "consumer feedback" is continuously cross-referenced with production-related data as well as information on the distribution and sales of goods and services. As a result, consumer feedback now incorporates transaction-generated information that specifies the time, place, and "means" of purchase (credit card, check, cash, rebate)—information that can be used to refine the circulation and promotion of products and services toward probable consumers. This networked "multilogue" between marketers, consumers, and products has been greatly enhanced by computer and database technology (Loro 1995).

Recently, scholars of new information and communication technologies (ICTs) have argued that the database is a new media form (Cubitt 2000, Manovich 1999, Poster 1991). We might even consider the database to be the unifying medium that binds together "multimedia" or computerized networks, particularly the personal computer and the Internet. Given the relatively decentered nature of the database, particularly compared to film and television, critics have tended to problematize traditional notions of authorship, narrative, and ownership (including intellectual property and copyright). Not surprisingly, many media and literary critics have argued that databases offer uniquely open-ended narrative possibilities, where readers inherently become writers and consumers become producers (Landow 1992). In other words, users read hyperlinked documents and also create links (and subsequent "paths," narratives, or stories) of their own making. However, as I have recently argued (Elmer 2001), database technologies today, particularly hypertext-enabled ones, increasingly redefine cultural production in decidedly passive terms. Likewise, simply "browsing" the Web is now frequently equated with producing or writing (Wakeford 2000). Similarly, with respect to the collection of personal information in consumer databases, individuals are now more apt to have their behaviors, likes, and dislikes *passively* (or perhaps *automatically*) integrated into proprietorial (commercial) databases than to decide (pro)actively and consciously to offer their personal information.

Historically, consumer information has nonetheless played a significant role in rationalizing the spheres of production, sales, and distribution. James Beniger's *The Control Revolution: Technological and Economic Origins of the Information Society* (1986), for example, traces the history and role of "mass feedback technologies" in American "commercial research" (the forerunner to marketing research). Early techniques of gathering customer feedback included magazine questionnaires (1914), house-to-house interviews (1916), attitude and opinion surveys (1929), indices of retail sales (1933), A. C. Nielsen's media-audiences measuring system (1935), and George Gallup's opinion poll (1936). And while researchers have used many of these techniques to question consumers about their likes and dislikes, recent attempts at gathering consumer intelligence have become increasingly more subtle and networked. Some would like to believe that responses to such solicitations have been largely voluntary, but the business sector— in its historical pursuit of full rationalization of all facets of business—has actively sought to automate the collection of personal information, increasingly within the very act of consumption. In short, the business sector has sought to bundle and automate the retail sale together with its solicitations for personal information from the consumer.

Of course, the bundling of solicitations into sales and increasingly other everyday "duties" (such as banking, making flight reservations, or renting a DVD or video) depended on a series of technological breakthroughs in computer technology. For example, the tabulation of demographic information in the ninth U.S. census (1870) offers an early glimpse into the power of collecting machine-readable data and of cross-referencing different sets of data to create increasingly timely demographic "pictures." Although the technologies used in that census were often described in objective, mathematics-related terms (such as *counting machines* or *tabulators*), they categorized statistics that reflected a population that had already been limited by sex and race. The process of collecting information, in other words, assumed a degree of demographic coding that did not accord equal value or status to the pool of possible respondents.

The value of such demographic relationships was later enhanced when information about commodities and services was integrated or cross-referenced with consumer or sales data, eventually leading to real-time data-management systems. Changes in any element of production, distribution, or sales could subsequently inform others. The digitization of inventories themselves would, in the form of early bar-coding technology, pave the way for the identification of mobile commodities (via bar codes) and consumers ("machine-readable" credit cards, discount memberships cards, and other forms of consumer identification cards). Thus, as commodities and consumer purchases could be traced and cross-referenced with geographic and temporal specificity, "point-of-sales" techniques began to sort consumers into taste groups, "clusters," or "profiles" to continuously suggest like-minded commodities and services.

THE AUTOMATION OF TABULATION: COUNTING AND CROSS-REFERENCING THE PEOPLE

> The word *census* comes from the Roman *censor*, an official responsible for the registration of citizens, evaluation of property, the spending of that revenue, and the guarding of public morals. The U.S. Bureau of the Census does the first task, and something of the second. But it is specifically prohibited from aiding in collecting taxes, and instead of guarding public morals census takers dutifully count households of unmarried couples—with no pointing of fingers. (Halacy 1980, 10)

In the above passage, law historian Dan Halacy implicitly champions the objectivity of the American census as a counting process whose workers make no moral assumptions as they "dutifully count households." However, the first American federal census was defined in article 1, section 2, of the U.S. Constitution as "the whole Number of free Persons, including those bound to Service for a Term of Years, and excluding Indian not taxed, three fifths of all other Persons." When President George Washington signed the census bill in March 1790, citizens therefore understood that the process would not be a objective count of heads that represented all inhabitants of the United States but, rather, that the population would be categorized along sexual and racial lines (Halacy 1980, 202).

The institutional and technological automation of such discriminatory practices was largely limited, however, until the ninth American census of 1870, when the chief clerk of the census,

Colonel Charles W. Seaton, designed a simple tabulating machine (Alterman 1969, 225). Seaton's system counted large numbers of census returns, but the age of diagnosable demography (meaning the study of data that can be efficiently counted and cross-referenced) was not fully realized until Herman Hollerith's punch-card tabulating machine (1890). Hollerith, later one of the founders of International Business Machines (IBM), constructed a system that had three main advantages over previous census counting machines. Hollerith's machine was efficient: it tabulated the results of the 1890 census approximately eight to ten times faster and twice as accurately as human beings had counted the results of the 1880 census. The punch-card tabulating machine also saved the government approximately $5 million (Alterman 1969, 225). As previously noted, though, the most important technological aspect of the tabulating machine was its ability to efficiently cross-tabulate items, making demographic profiles of particular groups based on relationships such as dwelling and income. Thus, according to an article published in *The Electrical Engineer* in 1891 (Martin 1891),

[Hollerith] saw that with increasing population and increasing complexity in data, the difficulties were becoming such that unless improved means of compilation were devised, the work must be abandoned in despair or become more incomplete and unsatisfactory each decade. On the other hand, with the aid of new facilities, not only might time and money be saved, but the data could be thrown into combinations full of suggestion and teaching, but which had been utterly beyond reach before. Such facilities Mr. Hollerith has furnished in his electric tabulating machine. The fundamental idea is ... to punch holes in cards so that the positions of these holes will correspond to certain data, and then to pass these cards through presses by which the perforations in the cards are made to control the operation of electromagnetics or groups of magnets, which in turn energize counting mechanism or sorting boxes, or will bring both into play at once.

As a forerunner to the modern computer, Hollerith's tabulating machine used technological logic that can be traced through census-taking and -tabulating technologies to the present day. For the 1940 census, for example, cross-referenced data from previous years were used to construct sample demographic groups that gave a statistically accurate profile of the entire nation. The technique of sampling allowed the census bureau to question only portions of the nation, saving a good deal of time and money in the process. According to Hyman Alterman (1969, 236), the 1940 census used sampling primarily to count and determine the domicile of army and navy veterans, the possession of Social Security numbers, and general details about regional occupations and industry.

Hollerith's techniques were further institutionalized within the U.S. Bureau of the Census with the acquisition of first-generation or UNIVAC I computers in 1951. Surprisingly, perhaps, the basic punch-card system devised by Hollerith was not replaced until the 1960 census, when the Film Optical Sensing Device for Input into Computers (FOSDIC) systems were operationalized. With the introduction of FOSDIC, enumerators merely transferred answers from individuals to a worksheet by filling in circles with pencils (Alterman 1969, 244).

With the introduction of third-generation computers in the early 1970s that were some 600 times more efficient than UNIVAC, the demographic information compiled by the U.S. government literally took on a life of its own in the Census Bureau's Data User Services Division (DUSD) (Halacy 1980, 56). Initially conceived as the marketing arm of the Census Bureau, DUSD received requests for data services from government officials, civic groups, charitable organizations, educators, students, and, significantly, market researchers (Halacy 1969, 181).

In addition to the census bureau's mandate to collect demographic data, though, overall American governmental support—in the form of new technologies and data services—for the business sector first emerged as a distinct and coherent policy in the early 1920s. Commerce Secretary Herbert Hoover was one of the first government officials to address the lack of coordination or even knowledge of the relationship among the spheres of production, distribution, and consumption. Hoover recognized that "No one had tried to properly trace the movement of a single commodity from manufacturer to consumer" (Leach 1993, 354). In the years preceding his presidential bid, Hoover successfully spearheaded the formation of the Bureau of Foreign and Domestic Commerce (BFDC). In conjunction with the Bureau of the Census and with partial funding from the U.S. Chamber of Commerce, the BFDC oversaw the first ever "consumption" census from 1926 to 1928. Reports from the census point to the topographical utility of such cross-referenced pieces of information, which provided the business sector with information on "how best to deliver goods, widen streets, construct parking lots and underground transportation, employ colored lights, foster store circulation, and present merchandise in 'tempting ways'" (Leach 1993, 365–366).

Philip M. Hauser's *Government Statistics for Business Use* (coedited with William R. Leonard, 1946) likewise offered over four hundred pages of in-depth analysis of government statistics and data related to manufacturing, agriculture, transportation, banking, housing, and national demographics. An early indicator of buying power, beyond land use and simple population count, could be found in the "Families: Income and Rent" index, which according to the index's creators, greatly assisted in the "Determination of Sales Areas and Quotas" (Hauser & Leonard 1946, 355). Hauser and Leonard also detailed the importance of sex, age, race, place of birth, and education in determining the market for products and services.

BUSINESS COMPUTERS IN "REAL TIME"

Although early tabulation technologies played a significant role in the collection and dissemination of demographic data by government departments working in conjunction with the U.S. Census Bureau, the networking of demographic databases within the spheres of production and inventory initially had to overcome the limitations of timeliness. As Norbert Wiener, James Carey, Harold Innis, and Armand Mattelart have all reminded us with the examples of the telegraph and the railway, new information technologies and techniques are often first applied to systems of transportation. The emergence of real-time computer technologies is in this regard no different. During the 1930s, American Airlines operated a centralized reservation system, dubbed the "Request and Reply" system, in which sales agents communicated via telephone with a centralized inventory control. This exceedingly slow process required a request for seating from a sales agent, a reply from inventory control, and finally a communication to the customer (Copeland, Mason & McKinney 1995). In response to the increasing numbers of Americans traveling by air after World War II, American Airlines installed the "Reservisor," a semiautomated reservation system, in its Boston office in 1946. Similar to Herman Hollerith's punch-card tabulating machine, the Reservisor operated through "a matrix of relays into which relays were manually inserted to indicate 'open' or 'closed.' . . . The columns of the matrix represented dates and the rows represented flight legs. . . . Checking the continuity between vertical and horizontal lines revealed whether a shorting plug had been inserted, meaning that a flight had been sold-out" (Copeland, Mason & McKinney 1995, 32–33).

An updated "Magnetronic Reservisor" system, fully installed in New York's LaGuardia Airport by 1952, further streamlined the process of scheduling and reservations. With the emergence of large Boeing 707 series of jetliners in the late 1950s, American Airlines worked closely with IBM executives and systems designers to customize a computer system for a much larger traveling public. Between 1960 and 1962, drawing on air defense systems previously built by IBM for the U.S. military, American and IBM programmers had built the Sabre automated airline reservation system and ushered in the era of computing in real time. By 1965, the Sabre system was fully online and had proven its capabilities in tracking complex schedules in real time for a number of other carriers, such as Delta Air Lines and Pan American World Airways (Copeland, Mason & McKinney 1995, 40).

Before such real-time tracking and inventory applications could be expanded into other areas of business and government, though, computer technology would have to address problems in data storage and cross-platform and -computer compatibility. While one could rightly conceive the punch card as among the first storage devices, the increased capacities of tape drive systems in the 1960s (including half-inch tape in IBM's System/360 and hyper-tape in IBM's 7340), advanced disk files, and removable disk packs (the size of phonograph records) made large amounts of data easily transported, stored, and diagnosed by compatible computers elsewhere (Pugh, Johnson & Palmer 1991). The innovation of such flexible storage and retrieval systems is largely attributed to John von Neumann and his colleagues at the Institute for Advanced Study's Computer Project at Princeton University from the years 1945 to 1947 (Richtmyer 1965).

Besides researching the arithmetic-grounded basis for machine language, the Institute for Advanced Study focused on the logic of storage units and memory. The Institute's applicability to contemporary computing and database systems lies in its discussion of assembler and compiler technologies. According to Richtmyer (1965), assembler and compilers formed the backbone of most coding mechanisms in the 1960s. He argues that "In [such] systems, the code is written, usually in somewhat symbolic form, in pieces, each of which ignores the other pieces; the assembler or compiler then puts the pieces together, assigns storage locations, and computes and inserts the relative addresses and the addresses of cross references between the pieces." Unlike the punch card or tape drive, which was inserted into the "tabulating machine," the accumulated data were located in the same device as the computer system data, which made possible the *continuous* and ongoing modification of programs during their actual operations, a logic that was later materialized in the hard drive of the personal computer (Richtmyer 1965, 10).

By 1952, increasingly powerful, automated, and affordable computer applications and information-tracking systems were entering the corporate and manufacturing business sectors. James W. Cortada (1996), for example, cites General Electric's installation of a digital computer in its Lexington, Kentucky, appliance factory as the first use of information technology in industrial production. Such an application, however, was quite unlike American Airline's reservation system in that it concentrated (initially, at least) on relatively simple accounting and inventory applications and (in the 1960s) on manufacturing resource-management applications. The ability to rationalize supply- and demand-based systems in a production, marketing, and consumption loop was not widely realized until both commodities and consumers were encoded with unique forms of identification—bar codes.

TRACKING AND INTEGRATING THE CONSUMER AND THE COMMODITY

Before consumer opinions could automatically be solicited within the production loop, however, products themselves (or "business inventories") would have to be incorporated into existing archival technologies. The Universal Product Code (UPC) provided the means by which individual commodities or larger shipments of products could be digitally coded through an imprint on packaging material. The UPC's preliminary applications in large supermarket chains in the 1970s were soon expanded to the inventory and shipping requirements of the U.S. Department of Defense and the auto industry in 1982.

The UPC consists of two sets of five-digit numbers below a series of machine-readable coded bars. The first set of numbers identifies the product's manufacturer, and the second set identifies the product's content (such as size, weight, and flavor) (Harrell, Hutt & Allen 1976). As Burke (1984, 1–2) reminds us, bar codes are therefore yet another means of storing data. They differ from punch cards or disks in that they are placed directly on commodities:

> Bar coding is a memory form. Printing black bars on white paper is directly analogous to recording plus or minus bars in a magnetic medium. In fact, the basic formats used in these two technologies are identical. While information recorded in magnetic media can be packed at higher densities, and can be erased and re-recorded, printing bar codes on plain paper is much less expensive for memory applications.

Another defining characteristic of the UPC (compared to earlier archival and tracking systems) is its use of optical character-recognition (OCR) technologies. Before the widespread adoption of UPC technology, inventories were categorized and tracked in very large quantities or were predetermined in easily quantifiable shipment sizes (such as the bushel or the dozen). OCR technology, however, could easily allow computer databases and other computer programs to scan letters and bar codes as digitized and individuated inventory information. The scannable bar code, in other words, facilitated the individual commodity's entrance into a larger computerized network or business loop. Moreover, OCR technology also introduced the storage capabilities of magnetic stripes onto personal identification cards, entering specific aspects of consumer behavior into computerized systems of inventory control, marketing, and sales and more closely tracking the ever elusive object of the niche-market researcher's desire—the consumer.

THE CONVERGENCE OF SOLICITATION AND SALES: POINT-OF-SALE TECHNOLOGIES

For consumers, this real-time and networked computer system of tracking inventory, sales, and consumer behavior is increasingly visible at the point of purchase (POP) or point of sale (POS). POP or POS advertising and marketing techniques are strategically placed in retail contexts. Point-of-purchase advertising, for instance, might include illuminated store front signs. Ben Menin, A. E. Benning, and Lee E. Benning (1992) also point to the double-sided curbside ice cream sign as a popular technique of retail advertising in the years preceding World War II. In the United States, wooden Indian statues similarly adorned the sidewalks in front of tobacconists from the years 1840 to 1880 (Offenhartz 1968). In contemporary retail sales, Menin, Benning, and Benning offer a hard sell of POP techniques by arguing that such in-store advertising frees up sales staff, who need not explain products to customers, and enhances the overall aesthetic or image of the store. In relation to larger marketing campaigns, Menin, Benning, and Benning (1992, 23–24) further note that point-of-purchase advertising also facilitates in-store live demonstrations or sampling of products.

Facilitated by UPC and OCR, point-of-purchase techniques were designed to save time and improve price accuracy at supermarket checkout stations (Ing & Mitchell 1994). In the past decade, however, point-of-purchase technologies have been employed for more than simple advertising and sales personnel matters. Employing magnetic-strip technology, Citicorp's POP system provides a scannable customer card for supermarket checkouts. Citicorp uses the collected data—the history of the consumer's purchases—in a subsequent direct-mailing program that includes customized coupons marked with a household ID (Birt & Cooper 1990). Catalina Marketing Corporation's point-of-purchase system offers coupons at the checkout station that are automatically customized to a consumer's buying habits. Catalina also offers its coupons on the Web (Gallagher 1996). Apart from checkout exchanges, point-of-purchase technologies also incorporate marketing campaign materials directly on or adjacent to products and services. "Display vehicles" such as props and dispensers, for instance, typically highlight a particular product in high-volume areas of stores. "Flagging devices" similarly hold or dispense coupons at eye level in aisles (Menin, Benning & Benning 1992, 150–159).

Ironically, one initial concern about the UPC and the computerization of inventory centered on consumer confusion over prices. With the removal of price labels, producers worried about retaining their customers, particularly given the increased availability of competing products and services (Harrell, Hutt & Allen 1976, 7). Today, however, wholesalers and distributors seem to complicate their bottom lines to automate customer feedback within demographic and psychographic databases. Direct TV's 18-inch digital satellite system, for instance, retails for an "end cost" of $49—that is, of course, after a consumer has purchased a one-year subscription package and mailed in a rebate coupon worth $50. The fundamental advantage to the cash-back mail-in coupon is that producers can construct their own consumer databases, thereby bypassing the marketing techniques of their retailers. Montgomery

Ward offered a sizable $50 mail-in rebate on many of its products. Long before receiving their rebate checks, however, consumers were mailed a questionnaire soliciting their opinions on the pricing, quality, and delivery of their purchase. Although one could argue that such solicitation techniques are not obligatory or fully automated, the high rebate amount certainly offers a strong incentive for a customer to provide demographic data. To a lesser degree, the customized questionnaire—with the name of the purchaser and the store and the date of purchase imprinted on the introductory page—reminds the consumer that the return of the questionnaire has its potential benefits: "Your opinion counts and could win you a big-screen TV! Completing this questionnaire and returning the postage-paid postcard, automatically enters you in a drawing to win a BIG-SCREEN TV."

Point-of-sales techniques and strategies such as coupon-based campaigns or warranty cards are directed toward building or maintaining a "relationship" with consumers. Deighton, Peppers, and Rogers (1994, 60–63) note that such "Retention programs try to keep customers loyal, [whereas] . . . reacquisition programs to try to retrieve customers who have defected." Examples of relationship-building programs include frequent-user programs (typically employing the aforementioned preferred-customer cards) wherein a consumer's habits are solicited in return for rebates or other promises of financial return through sweepstakes and lotteries. Affinity clubs likewise attempt to foster an ongoing relationship with the consumer by offering specialized product services and advice. Kraft Foods, for example, provides the members of its Kraft Cheese and Macaroni Club a quarterly magazine entitled *What's Hot.*

Thus, such customer-retention enterprises and campaigns, often facilitated by point-of-purchase techniques and technologies, largely avoid sending advertising messages to consumers who most likely (statistically speaking) have absolutely no interest in (or ability to afford) a particular product or service. Outside the spaces of consumption and sales, however, the "misdirection" of advertising is still commonplace. Moreover, this "waste" or failure of advertising is not simply akin to some objective "sacrifice" that customers make in getting products not of their liking or desire. Rather, it represents the producer's failure to reach a probable consumer. Since cost inhibits the individuation of advertising messages, market research has—since its earliest manifestations in the early twentieth century—focused on searching for and capitalizing on particular consumers. Yet how are such markets identified?

While the nation-state is founded on abstract conceptions of citizenry, the techniques used to manage populations (and international relations) have always required knowledge of the available human and physical resources. Thus, citizens have always been required to contribute to a demographic knowledge base, in the form of a census, with census avoiders being subject to a penalty of fine or imprisonment. Hollerith reminds us, though, that as the tasks of governmentality became increasingly more complicated, they required faster and more efficient means of collecting, storing, and diagnosing data. The lasting utility of Hollerith's tabulating machine was its ability to rationalize relationships between pieces of data and thereby provide condensed pictures or profiles of particular groups and places. The widespread use of statistics in the 1940s further introduced techniques of sampling into processes of solicitation.

With a census taking place every decade, the U.S. government continues to archive and disseminate a seemingly incomprehensible amount of information. The government and many of its arm's-length apparatuses (particularly the military) have provided a good deal of leadership in the area of technological innovation. Complementing its function as provider of data services, the government has facilitated computerized data analysis of consumer marketing practices in production, advertising, distribution, and sales. Foremost in this regard is the application of real-time database technologies in the airline industry, which enable the immediate storage, retrieval, and updating of passenger and scheduling data. The convergence of storage and diagnosis technologies in computers (as software programs) subsequently facilitated the ongoing computation of relationships between changing inventories, sales, and consumer demographics and psychographics.

While the need to make immediate changes to databases is restricted to large-scale or emergency service providers such as government and transportation, the cross-referencing of inventories and consumer demand is also of prime importance for wholesalers and retailers. Implementing a strategy similar to that used by the airline industry, with the assistance of digital technologies such as Universal Product Codes (bar codes and coded "swipe" cards), the retail sector has incorporated inventory tracking within sales decisions. Unlike the airline industry, though, the retail and wholesale sales industries involve a wide array of commodities, and for businesses to remain profitable and competitive, managers must devise strategies to solicit psychographic profiles of consumers that predict their likelihood to be interested in product X, Y, or Z.

As this chapter has discussed, a key element in rationalizing overall business decisions and in discriminating consumers into niche markets is the technological automation of demographic and psychographic data. A distinguishing element of the sales transaction is the production and exchange of transaction-generated information (history of a consumer's buying habits) in return for a financial rebate or a promise of reward. Money, in other words, is not simply exchanged for products or for libidinal gratification, for that matter. Once a larger pool of transaction-generated information has been cross-referenced and tabulated in consumer databases, profiles are used to target probable consumers at home (via direct mailing) or at the cash register (customized coupons). Market researchers are interested in finding out what the customer wants, but they also want to use data on consumer behavior to foster, automate, and network the act of consumption.

By tracing the emergence of automated computer and information technologies into the spheres of production, promotion, and wholesale and retail sales, this chapter has argued that consumer feedback has increasingly become an integral part of ongoing, real-time (and just-in-time) technological loops. And as these strategies become more pervasive and automated, they subsequently become less distinguishable from the act of purchasing or (keeping in mind the tactics of coupon rebates and bar-coded supermarket cards) getting a "good deal." Such feedback does not simply inform the production of commodities, offering objective input on desired products for individual consumers. Rather, feedback techniques are often used to cluster like-minded consumers together so that their aggregate purchases—and hence psychographics—can be cross-referenced with production, distribution, and sales data. As is shown in the next chapter's discussion of geographical information systems (GIS), the cross-referencing of data is often spatialized and mapped (just as Herbert Hoover intended with the first consumption census) to give industries in the private sector the intelligence required to reconfigure their operations to maximize their relationships to specific clusters of consumers. The mapping of consumer profiles in the context of the marketing and sales of products and services thus enters the domain of prescribing or otherwise governing spatial relationships.

4

[Computers] simulate surveillance in the sense that they precede and redouble the means of observation. Computer profiling ... is understood best not just as a technology of surveillance, but as a kind of surveillance in advance of surveillance, a technology of "observation before the fact." (Bogard 1996, 27)

Few would argue that the debate over postmodernity, and in particular the concept of simulation, has been dominated by the works of—and polemics surrounding—media and social theorist Jean Baudrillard. While clearly benefitting from the Baudrillardian oeuvre, William Bogard's *The Simulation of Surveillance: Hypercontrol*

MAPPING PROFILES

in Telematic Societies (1996) turns to Michel Foucault and Gilles Deleuze to discuss technological changes in the information economy. Focusing on questions of effect and process, Bogard investigates the dynamics of the cybernetic process or the means by which information systems reconstitute themselves. As is shown in chapter 2, Foucault is useful to the extent that he introduces the significance of a repressive, automated system of surveillance. Bogard (1996, 26) attempts to redress the limitations of such a model by insisting that simulations are "projected onto something." Simulations are, in other words, a result of a particular diagnostic process that stresses the power of visualizing past, present, and possible future topographical relationships. For Bogard, bodies are consequently codified, and sites of confinement give way to a ubiquitous "society of control."

Whereas chapter 3 discusses the emerging networking capabilities of particular computer technologies over the course of the twentieth century, this chapter offers a more technical and systematic discussion of personal information. And where chapter 3 provides background about emerging technological innovations that *automated* consumer desires and opinions into a production, sales, and distribution loop, this chapter discusses the manner in which personal information is first collected and networked into computer systems and then cross-referenced, profiled, and continuously *simulated* in the form of computer maps. By focusing on the importance of geographic data and mapping technologies, this chapter critiques the architectural tendencies in Foucaultian studies of personal information. In so doing, the chapter offers an example of a diagrammatic system of production that attempts to map and henceforth govern consumers, markets, and spaces.[1]

Through a discussion of the modes and modulations of "data acquisition"—the construction, diagnosis, and applicability of consumer databases—I again note that consumer "surveillance" is predicated on the active solicitation of personal information from individuals in exchange for the promise of some form of reward. Through the act of browsing, exchanging, requesting, and consuming, individual consumers actively assist in the reproduction of consumer markets. Yet this process does not start or stop with solicitation, automated or otherwise. Rather, consumer profiles are constructed through cross-referencing various categories of data (demographic, psychographic, geographic, and so on). Geocoding consumer databases, computer-simulated maps, and geographical information systems (GIS) can infinitely reproduce updated maps of markets, a process that increasingly facilitates the forecasting and governmentalization of the human, economic, and political topography.

THE MODULATION OF INFORMATION

With a decidedly topographical focus, this chapter responds to recent influential analyses of the information economy offered by the likes of Oscar Gandy and Mark Poster by operationalizing Michel Foucault and Gilles Deleuze's thoughts on power, space, and the diagram-as-map. Gandy and Poster—two seemingly radically incommensurate scholars—share a common affinity with the notion of "dataveillance" (the surveillance of a population through database technologies). Although Gandy and Poster offer compelling arguments based on their political, economic, and theoretical studies of consumer surveillance technologies, I discuss the segmentation and storage of consumer profiles in databases and argue that both authors downplay the significance of soliciting and mapping consumer behavior.

Contemporary discussions and debates over the nature of technological systems are not restricted to the academy. For example, some in the business sector have described the database as a "smart" technological apparatus "which drives an intelligence or learning process that provides information for marketing decision making." (Jackson & Wang 1994, 29). The language of architecture tends to appear in the growing body of literature on database technologies. David Martin (1991, 24), for instance, describes the process of formatting, accumulating, and coding data as drawing on "relational architectures." But that language all too often stops short of a reflexive system of data production. In other words, such critiques fail to address the means by which information is consistently and repetitively updated and mapped via computer programs such as GIS, or they limit such assessments and diagnoses to the realm of the indexical (for example, as lists).

As previously mentioned, I would loosely classify such approaches under the heading "dataveillance," as initially defined by computer scientist Roger A. Clarke (1994, 122–123):

> [Dataveillance is] automated monitoring through computer readable data rather than physical observation.... Dataveillance is the systematic use of personal data systems in the investigating and monitoring of the actions or communications of one or more persons.

Clarke's contribution to the study of surveillance (and what distances his work from more literal-minded readings of panopticism) is his recognition of the dispersal of such technologies—their ability to survey behavior "from a distance." Yet what remains at best unclear in Clarke's discussion of dataveillance is the degree to which personal information relates to—indeed, fuels and regenerates—techniques and technologies that solicit, diagnose, store, and map personal information.

Mark Poster's (1990, 75) investigation of database technologies likewise privileges language over sight within the indexical architectures of the database. As a result, Poster (1990, 69) argues that in comparison to the example of television,

> The database represents a somewhat different language situation. In this case the individual is not addressed at all; he or she receives no messages. Rather the communication goes the other way around. The individual, usually indirectly, sends messages to the database. In one sense the database is nothing more than a repository of messages.

Unfortunately, as is evidenced in this quotation, the process of soliciting and collecting information into databases is characterized by Poster as a one-way flow from the consumer to the database.

Perhaps Poster is being overly literal in his writing, arguing for a more rigid system of control where individuals have little to no agency.

Consumer databases clearly do speak to individuals, often in the form of targeted solicitations. Everyday routines or interactions in a consumer society are also wrought with numerous technologies of solicitation (such as supermarket rebate-card "swipes," credit-card transactions, and video rentals) that by design attempt to automate the solicitation of personal information in exchange for varying degrees and manifestations of reciprocity (including pleasure, cash discounts, and prizes). Dataveillance's focus on the database has also in large part been technologically surpassed by the recent innovations in computer technology and telecommunications, manifested in increasingly interconnected computer systems—a veritable convergence of technologies that accumulate, code, and most important map personal information.

DATA SOLICITATION

The moment of solicitation—as a particular form of exchange—is characterized by a divulgence of personal information in return for varying degrees of pleasure or the possibility or promise of financial rebates, cash prizes, holiday cruises, and so on (as chapter 5 shows, this exchange often takes place when the individual enters a contest, draw, or lottery). Whereas this book has focused primarily on the influential panopticon chapter of Michel Foucault's *Discipline and Punish: The Birth of the Prison* (1977), other treatments of consumer culture such as Rick Maxwell's (1996a, 1996b) have turned to Foucault's *The History of Sexuality: An Introduction* (1978) to explicate the reciprocal and (self) governmental dimensions of information exchange. Maxwell's (1996b, 107) studies of market researchers (or interviewers) as quasi-ethnographers[2] characterize the human interaction between market researcher and consumer as a form of "confessional," albeit in more secular terms. For Foucault, the act of confession reinforces a mode of governmentality that requires individuals to routinely articulate their loquacious desires and transgressions. To elicit such "confessionals," the market researcher must gain the confidence of the interviewee through a relationship based on a mutually respectful reciprocity. The desire for interviewees to confess to enjoying a certain product or service—in the hopes that their lifestyles will be "represented" in future commodities and market decisions—must, in other words, be "rewarded" with an understanding or supportive response on the part of the researcher or with a promise of financial reward. Hence, Maxwell (1996b, 107–108) argues, market researchers in this capacity

> listen to stories about people's relation to every imaginable kind of product, from household cleaners to perfumes and flight attendants. Market researchers interpret these stories as local assessments about the value people ascribe to goods and services, reporting what they find to corporate clients wishing to improve merchandising techniques in as many different markets as possible. . . . The market researcher furnishes a place for people to report their beliefs and opinions, doubts and successes, gossip on the streets rumors from the neighbors. This secular confessional is the first station supplying the human face to global products.

Maxwell's comments on the role of the market researcher are helpful because they broaden the definition of consumer solicitation—in this instance, to a transnational and "front-line" dialogic moment. However, when Maxwell (1996a, 222) argues that "the perceived innocuousness of the encounter of course does not eliminate domination; it just distances and ex-nominates the political economy," he nonetheless fails to relate the confessional as "technology of the self" (as self-discipline) to the reproduction of other more automated and ubiquitous consumer technologies. The process of solicitation is, as such, but one element in the reproduction of consumer markets and topographical relationships.

And just as techniques of solicitation come in various shapes and sizes (some exceedingly blatant and obtrusive, others banal and ubiquitous) in their bid to address the predictability and routinization of particular consumers and markets, likewise, not all personal information collected is of the same stock and utility. Rather, as raw materials for market researchers, various categories of data become integral elements in the diagnostic process—that is, the means by which information is cross-referenced. In *Lifestyle Market Segmentation*, Ronald D. Michman (1991) outlines four primary categories of data. First, geographic data encompass categories such as region, climate, population density, and market area. Examples of geographic data include telephone area codes, zip codes, and Internet URLs and domain names. Second, demographic data tend to focus on personal information that is specific and unique to an individual. Examples of demographic data include age, sex, race, marital status, income, occupation, education, religion, race, and nationality. Third, psychographic data attempt to address social aspects such as class, values, lifestyles, and personality. Finally, consumer behavior data refers to specific needs and desires, such as usage rate, brand loyalty, product knowledge, and attitude about specific products.

Each of Michman's categories of data serves a distinct role in the diagnosis of commercial markets and consumer behavior. Demographic data often serve as a baseline of relatively consistent and easily understood statistics (we change our domicile much less than we change our tastes for commodities and services such as restaurants, for instance). Demographic data also distinguishes us as individuals to such an extent that this type of information serves as fodder for everyday small talk ("How old is your baby?" "When is your birthday?") and for increasingly common solicitations or exchanges over the phone, online, or at the checkout counter ("May I have your last name, please?"). Thus, demographic data might seem to serve as a powerful means of surveying and tracking individuals, but its purpose in diagnosing and profiling consumers is largely restricted to a baseline function: demographic data often serve as the object rather than the subject of consumer database marketers. By comparison, psychographic data often blurs the distinction between object and subject positions by both categorizing values (object) and potentially changing or modifying values (subject). This process is then crystallized in consumer behavior data (which can be conceived of as an individual's overall lifestyle), where for the purposes of expanding and reconstituting markets, notions of use value and brand loyalty are actively and constantly in need of reformation.

The process of data acquisition for consumer databases operates via numerous techniques, technologies, and places, yet one commonality that unites these disparate attempts at solicitation is the need for the collected data to be codified and profiled—typically the transformation of actions, habits, and behaviors (in short, lifestyles) into a simple system of classification. Faye W. Gilbert and William E. Warren (1995, 229), for example, classify consumer profiles into a number of types. The "economizer," for instance, is a profile (the sum of data cross-referenced to give a picture) for an individual who is likely to shop for specials. Not surprisingly, the "credit user" is a profile for those likely to use credit for almost all purchases. The more abstract "self-confident" profile refers to individuals who perceive themselves as independent minded. The "home oriented" profile is used for those who are interested in domestic technologies (particularly entertainment) and who "would rather spend a quiet night at home than go to a party." And finally, the "fashionable" profile is constructed for those who believe that it is important to "dress smartly."

Such consumer profiles form the backbone of contemporary marketing research—the categorization of "probable" consumers based on patterns of past behavior. Yet consumer profiles alone remain ineffective without the introduction and diagnosis of geographic data. Geographical data allow marketers to rationalize and henceforth make efficient everyday communication and circulation of information in the nation-state (such as zip codes in mail delivery) and spatially anchor data collected from more routinized technologies of solicitation (such as credit-card purchases and videotape rentals). These are critical points that Gandy, for example, largely avoids in his Foucaultian analysis of the information economy. In other words, Gandy's "Panopticon Sort" (1993, 10) logically mirrors Jeremy Bentham's (1995) panoptic prison and Michman's (1991) previous three modes of indexical apparatuses in that it

> serves as a powerful metaphorical resource for representing the contemporary technology of segmentation and targeting, which involves surveillance of consumers, their isolation into classes and categories, and their use in market tests that have the character of experiments.

Thus, without visualizing consumer databases in graphical or iconic models, marketers can only attempt to integrate strategies of marketing with the actual delivery of commodities and services and therefore are limited in their ability to govern or prescribe spatial reformation. Taking the example of zip codes (or political jurisdictions, such as counties or school districts, or telephone area codes) in computer databases, it is important to distinguish between coding space and categorizing or coding lifestyle and consumer habits. In the former, we are still "segmenting" in the

Foucaultian sense: we are distinguishing between this and that particular quality. Such an argument is, for example, clearly at work in Foucault's (1986, 23) thoughts on demography in situs, as opposed to a topology of psychographics or lifestyle:

> The problem of siting or placement arises for mankind in terms of demography. This problem of the human site or living space is not simply that of knowing whether there will be enough space for men in the world—a problem that is certainly quite important—but also that of knowing what relations of propinquity, what type of storage, circulation, marking, and classification of human elements should be adopted in a given situation in order to achieve a given end. Our epoch is one in which space takes for us the form of relations among sites.

TECHNOLOGIES OF MAPPING: GEOGRAPHIC INFORMATION SYSTEMS

> Maps existed, of course. . . . they were maps that were drawn by hand and every time a minor change occurred they had to be redone by hand, a tediously slow process (Rundles 1992, 41).

Geographical information systems (GISs) are essential components in the electronic mapping of information. This powerful desktop computer software introduces a degree of reflexibility to the maintenance and updating of consumer databases. The term *GIS*, however, has historically referred to varying modes or models of spatial analysis rather than to any one particular computer program or product. John Pickles (1995, 3), for instance, argues that GIS has at one time or another been used to refer to or describe a field of interdisciplinary researchers; a particular "community"; "an approach to geographic inquiry and spatial data handling; a series of technologies for collecting, manipulating, and representing spa-

tial information; a way of thinking about spatial data; a commodi-
fied object that has monetary potential and value; and a technical
tool that has strategic value."

Land-based GIS, operationalized in the maintenance, modification, and diagnosis of personal information, however, dates back to
the early 1970s resource management in Colorado. As a pioneer in
geodemographic mapping, the state's leading utility officer, Del-
win D. Hock, has been widely acknowledged as a pioneer in the
field of GIS. Hock offers the reasoning behind his efforts to diagnose geographic data (Parent & Konty 1992, 20):

> All the [computer] emphasis had been on accounting and
> billing.... But I thought, How do we better utilize the
> excess capacity? Geography is a very important part of our
> business.... Every facility and customer has a unique geo-
> graphical location. I thought, How do we create a computer
> model of that system?

The chair realized his goal of a geographical information program
by joining geographic and spatial information where his customers
were located in relation to the company's services.

Although GIS technologies were largely relegated to large corporations and government agencies in the 1980 and early 1990s, their
ability to cross-reference past patterns to prescribe or simulate
future relationships—facilitated by an increase in speed, accuracy,
and depth in "mappable" information, drastically decreased consumer prices, and widespread personal computer compatibility—
has benefitted a range of activities in both the marketplace and the
civic arena. In mapping or visualizing "what-if" scenarios, for
example, campaigns could pretest products, services, campaign
slogans, promotions, and advertisements on present and future
geographic communities. In this capacity, GIS can be viewed as
"simulational as well as representational" (Goss 1995, 182).

> It is ... subsumed and amassed cultural capital that map-
> making societies bring to the task of making maps; not the
> patiently acquired mastery of this or that individual more or
> less carefully passed on—often in secret—through speech or
> gesture or inculcated habit. It is the endlessly reproduced and
> everywhere disseminated wisdom of thousands of such indi-
> viduals, caught up, stored, annotated, corrected, indexed,
> epitomized, reduced to formulae, taught by rote, so that
> what once was an epochal discovery or invention is reduced
> to common knowledge, grounded into a taken-for-granted
> fact of life. (Wood 1992, 48)

In attempting to rethink database technology (and dataveillance)
within the context of computer networks, solicitation techniques,
and information mapping software, information is consistently
updated in a cybernetic or cyclical fashion—a process that is
heightened by its constant production of graphic representations of
space (maps). Although one could rightly argue on purely technological grounds that computerized maps can condense data more
efficiently than database outputs or that the power of maps stems
from their representational status as iconic, easily recognizable
signs, such approaches nevertheless fail to account for the reflexive
element of reproduction, spurred on by the need to accumulate
increasingly more precise data profiles. Geocoding psychographics
from a database, for example, is essential for successful mail-order
campaigns (catalogues), yet at the same time there is no absolute
requirement to view (in the graphical sense of the term) the
addresses and geographical entity in question (that is, the topographical market). As such, this indexical approach could be interpreted as making a clear distinction between human features and
topological characteristics: "It is important to understand that geo-

coding software applications do not require a mapping system [such as GIS]. A geocoder simply reads data, analyzes the address specific portion of the data, and then attempts to match each address with a location, a latitude and longitude" (MapInfo 1995, 3).

The introduction of computer maps by GIS, however, calls into question this "split" between human and geographic data—a bifurcation often characterized by empirical and scientific claims. In other words, traditionally (Martin 1991, 4–5),

> data relating to dynamic human populations are very different in their geographic properties to those relating to the physical world: the location of any individual is almost always referenced via some other spatial object, such as a household address or a census data collection unit. Unlike a road intersection or a mountain summit, we are rarely able to define the location of an individual simply by giving their map reference.

Thus in addition to the obvious claims of efficiency and "clarity" —to the extent that GIS produces pictures of relationships— such computer maps also enter into a search for empirical or "true" representations of both the geographic and human world. Given the inherent problems in predicting human behavior and the ever-changing environment (natural and human), we might ask ourselves how an accurate picture is ever achieved. One answer (to return to the cybernetic qualities of diagrammatic thinking) is by cleaning. According to the Group 1 Software corporation, "Dirty data is the number one cause behind inaccurate mapping analysis" (MapWorld 1996, 5). In the case of the database, then, the process of capturing the world "out there" must be up to date. It cannot be missing a zip code, or consumer promotions, political campaign material, and state documents would never reach their desired locations. Computer "cleansing" programs such as those marketed by Group 1 locate the correct addresses while also attempting to reconstruct an accurate and "true" representation of the world's topography. In this respect, one could view "the dirt" (or incorrect data) as what escapes initial attempts at "cleaning" (because it is miscoded or misformatted), hence driving the never-ending cycle toward pure, white, clean data—the accurate representation of human topography.

THE LAYERING OF (E)MOTION

Advances in satellite technologies over the past ten to twenty years have also facilitated an ideology of topographical and human "cleanliness." Apart from providing unobstructed views, satellite technologies also accumulate previously unattainable data through various means and modes of acquisition. Satellite remote sensing, however, no longer utilizes simple photographic (meaning purely visual) lenses to capture views of the earth's surface. The first American satellites, in operation by the National Space and Aeronautics Administration (NASA) 1960, did operationalize rudimentary television-type cameras to photograph the rotation and surface of the earth. Due to the limitations imposed by the cloud cover that obscures the earth's surface, later satellites used multisensorial technologies such as "the Advanced Very High Resolution Radiometer, a High Resolution Infrared Sounder, . . . a Stratospheric Sounder Unit, a Microwave Sounder Unit, a Data Collection System, and a Space Environment Monitor" (Mapworld 1996, 49).

While recent satellite technologies offer ground resolution anywhere from eight to thirty meters, drawn from radiation emissions from the earth's surface (Martin 1991, 20), the widespread use of global positioning systems have perhaps more than any other previous technology introduced a near perfect device for pinpointing

and mapping any point on the earth's surface. The empirical claims
of such systems offer a much stronger cleaning solution for the
muddied data terrain.

Born of the U.S. Department of Defense (DOD),[3] GPS facilitates an exactitude in geographical mapping that was previously
unimagined in the history of technology. With a hand-held computer, an individual can at any time draw on twenty-four radio-
emanating GPS satellites positioned some 19,100 kilometers above
the earth's surface to obtain their precise longitude and latitude
coordinates (Mapworld 1996). Available in the United States for
approximately $150, according to the U.S.-based GIS corporation
MapInfo, "GPS Technology is ideal for real-time tracking such
as fleet management and 911 response, and for field data collection such as rural addressing. Many municipalities now gather this
information from a combination of tax maps, aerial photographs,
and odometer readings. GPS greatly simplifies this task because it is
now possible to plot precise positions and input them directly into
a computer to create a real-time database" (Mapworld 1996, 16).

Drawing on everyday, networked consumer-solicitation technologies, GPS, and other remote sensing technologies (from surveillance planes to satellite imaging), computer programs such as GIS
thus attempt to account for changes in both the physical and psychographic worlds. The layering of such processes in the form of
maps is moreover in constant motion, informed and updated by
the ever-changing human condition (new addresses, roads, housing projects, and so on). Once geocoded, the emotive investments
of the populace—the likes, dislikes, and desires of demographic
groups—can be located, capitalized on, in the case of incorrect
data "cleansed," or most important forecasted in space. In comparing this process of layering (e)motion (in the form of a diagram
map) with "hinged-flap" maps that are laid over top each other,
Phil Parent and Larry Konty (1992, 26) conclude that the

"concept of showing spatial and temporal change by overlays is a crucial underpinning of GIS."

CONCLUSIONS

As particular machines that simulate time and space relations, simulation maps that enable one to locate, rationalize, prescribe, and hence govern the spatial patterns of consumerism and everyday life can be conceived of as documents both in and for action. In technological terms, while GIS and database technologies are both useful in finding markets, I would like to suggest that the ability to layer data in the form of a simulation (map) affords a particular diagnostic and hence governmental capacity—that is, a process that integrates variables in a forecasting mode or inquiry. For the commercial sector, this "layering" of data (in the form of a map) enables individuals and companies to locate future profitable sites and travel routes based in large part on their geographic proximity to (among other factors) markets, means of transportation, adequate energy sources, and trained "human resources." In short, the visualizing of geographic data "anchors," albeit in simulational terms, the movement of goods and services, thus providing coordinates from which one may plot such entrepreneurial strategies.

Although I have taken some steps to distance the machinations of GIS mapping from database technologies—particularly in highlighting the manner in which the former draws on overwhelmingly empirical definitions and representations of topography—it is only by returning to the level of the everyday that we can begin to talk about the rationalization of the human topography. In other words, psychographic data on consumer behavior are accumulated by way of numerous "solicitations" of interactivity that are most explicitly manifest in the face-to-face questions posed by the market researcher but also less obviously (but increasingly and pervasively) present in the everyday performative duties required of commodity purchasing. The consumer therefore appears to be governed by a logic of representation that manifests itself in the exchange of personal information in return for (promised) financial rebate. The power of such marketing strategies and techniques thus lies in facilitating the process of consumption and "confession" all at once: research and sales become one in the same, informing each other's rules, regulations, and practices.

Such practices are also manifested by their situation or placement in spatial patterns and routines. In this respect, one can literally trace the spatial patterns of a consumer's behavior from the residual trail left behind by his or her purchases. David Lyon (1994, 52) thus rightly argues that there is a

> tendency for surveillance systems increasingly to depend on their subjects to trigger their activity, by means of a trail of transactional information left behind as we make purchases of phone calls, submit claims, or state preferences.

Retracing these trails of data is not the only research function that gives GIS its unique power in the strategies of marketing. Rather, the layering of (e)motion engenders in topological terms a reflexive drive toward both mapping and prescribing particular markets in space. Although I have discussed the layering of motion in largely custodial terms (as the technological cycle of "cleaning dirt"—for example, in GPS remote sensing), the layering of emotion (defined as behaviors, likes, dislikes—in short, lifestyle) on top of space provides the diagrammatic link to governing or prescribing the very routes and time-space paths that afford our everyday needs, wants, desires, and duties. Such attempts to map are not merely representational; they are an ongoing attempt to govern the topography of everyday lifestyles.

5

On almost every day of the year, New York City's Grand Central Station bustles with office workers and tourists who pass strategically positioned street signs, maps, cafés, newspaper stands, and wall-to-wall advertisements of every shape, size, and color. Increasingly ubiquitous iconic signs or corporate logos (such as Nike's "check mark" logo or Pepsi's red, white, and blue circle) likewise seem to meld into every facet of our lives, littering the eye-level horizon of our everyday "time-space paths" (Harvey 1989). But the fragmentation or interruption of such commercial placements and messages has also become increasingly commonplace. During a typical rush hour in Grand Central Station, for instance, the top-selling tequila in the United States, José Cuervo,

DEPLOYING PROFILES IN PROMOTIONAL EVENTS

sponsored Octuba Fest 1993, a concert of over a hundred tubas. In an interview with the trade journal *Brandweek*, a José Cuervo vice president posed this question: "Consumers can either flip through a magazine looking at ads, or they can be dancing to tequila songs played on a tuba.... Which do you think they'd rather do?" (Warner 1994, 18).

London-based Virgin likewise attempted to mirror the successful concert promotions of Scotland's Tennent Caledonian Breweries by hosting the V96 Festival (held in Chelmsford, England). Both Virgin and Tennent used the concerts as promotional devices to reach a particular market segment by associating their products with top British acts and the concert experience itself (Marsh & Lee 1996, 10).

While such large-scale promotions complicate the conventions of traditional media advertising (print, radio, and television) and, spatially, the rhythms of everyday life, their marketing goals are not always limited to heightened product visibility or to niche-market association. Denmark's Fris Vodka, for example, is one of many brands that are attempting to chip away at the dominance of Sweden's Absolut Vodka in the American market. It has promoted a number of "mini-events" such as gallery openings or charity events. At each event, the Fris "Style Demo Team" distributes free vodka and solicits demographic information from partygoers in return for redeemable Fris Vodka "checks." The initial campaign provided Fris with a fifteen-hundred-name consumer database (Warner 1994, 19). For companies such as Fris, then, event marketing and sponsorships provide an opportunity to target, solicit (research), and advertise to a specific market.

The José Cuervo Octuba Fest, Virgin's V96 Festival, and the Fris mini-events are examples of how the advertising industry routinely addresses the limitations of print advertisements, billboards, television commercials, and other recall-based advertising campaigns. The relative demise of recall-based advertising is not an entirely new phenomenon, however. As early as 1980, for example, the advertising industry began phasing out mnemonic jingles in advertising campaigns, even though the jingle had long been used for consumer recall (Goldman & Parson 1994, 24). In its place, the industry began to develop the promotion of events—or "event marketing"—by large corporations as an essential element of promotional campaigns. According to *Brandweek*, by the mid-1980s, event marketing was an $800 million business in the United States, and ten years later, it had grown into a $4.5 billion industry. Because marketing executives like to reduce their varied techniques to simple catch words such as "linkage advertising" and "micro-marketing," they tend to include a wide array of marketing campaigns under the heading of "event marketing." Not surprisingly, sports, music, fairs, "causes," and "arts" top the list of events that corporations tend to favor. The top sponsors of event marketing in the United States are Philip Morris, Anheuser-Busch, Coca-Cola, Eastman Kodak, General Motors, IBM, RJR Nabisco, PepsiCo, and AT&T (Warner 1994, 24).

Although the marketing industry typically differentiates campaigns by event and cost, the sponsoring company also needs to organize the event and integrate market research techniques into the event. For example, a single sponsor does not organize telecasts of the popular *Monday Night Football* on ABC in the United States, even though the game relies heavily on its many sponsors: sponsors come and go, but the game goes on. Events such as the V96 Festival, conversely, are exclusively organized by a single corporation (in this instance, Virgin). Such exclusivity has costs and benefits. What happens to the sales and image of a brand, for example, if the event turns out to be a disaster? On a more positive side, exclusive event-marketing promotions offer complete control of imagery and potential tie-ins with promotional campaigns and consumer research.

Whatever the variation, such events have become a common anchor in a larger sales, marketing, advertising, and distribution ("just-in-time") loop that is increasingly driven by the search for *consumer profiles* (a set of psychographic and demographic characteristics that suggest a "probable" consumer). Examples of event marketing thus offer a crystalized case study on integrating consumer variables (psychographics and demographics) into marketing decisions, events, broadcasts, and advertisements. As is shown in the two marketing events discussed in this chapter (Bass Ale's *Titanic*-related sweepstakes and Molson's "Polar Beach Party"), consumers not only are solicited for personal information but actually become part of the promotional enterprise itself. Sweepstakes winners participate in an event that is filmed and later incorporated into print, television, and online advertising and promotional materials.

In addition to offering a cybernetic perspective on the reproduction of consumer markets, this chapter also highlights the topographical implications of consumer profiling and event marketing. Instead of simply relying on static advertisements to convey commercial messages, event-marketing and profiling campaigns increasingly collect consumer "intelligence" (data on consumer behavior) that helps advertisers refine their commercial appeals and find advantageous *spaces of promotion*. By learning more about their probable consumers, corporations now routinely attempt to track and geographically map their markets. As previously noted, such geodemographic technologies suggest advantageous sites to sell products and collect more data on consumers.

As is evident in the example of Molson's Polar Beach Party, such events also disrupt the routinized codes (narratives, sizes, shapes, time, and sites) of everyday advertising. And as corporations increasingly compete for the attention (and data profiles) of consumers, event marketing has begun to mirror trends in the tourist industry (ecotourism, for example) by situating marketing events in unusual, out-of-the way, exotic, and *extreme* spaces and places—those geographically marginalized places that are rarely, if ever, widely associated with capital and consumption. In addition to the broad environmental questions that such events raise, their relatively homogeneous consumer profiles also raise questions about racial discrimination and profiling. What happens to those individuals, groups, communities, and nations that don't "fit the profile" for such events, contests, and products? The promotional endeavors of Molson highlight this question of identifying consumers on the basis of national identity as Molson has consistently associated itself with Canadian history, geography, politics, culture, and identity.[1] Before moving to questions of space, territory, and nationality, let us first examine the multimediated nature of consumer profiling and event marketing.

BASS ALE: BRINGING IT ALL BACK HOME

Faced with competitive domestic and international markets, an advertising firm working for England's Bass Brewers recently sought to align Bass Ale with authenticity, heritage, and history ("Bass' Titanic Mission" 1996). Building on its customers' desire for customized, unique, and "extreme" experiences and places, the firm tied its advertising campaign to one of the most glamorous tragedies of the twentieth century—the sinking of the *Titanic*. The public's seemingly limitless fascination with the loss of the "unsinkable" luxury liner has led to numerous portrayals of the sinking on television, on IMAX, on the stage, and in film. The ship has mesmerized cultural critics for decades and came to once again dominate the popular media when its sunken remains were located in the North Atlantic in the mid-1980s. With a longevity outlasting any natural disasters (such as tidal waves, earthquakes, tornados, or killer asteroids) that have been featured in Hollywood films and television movies, the wreck of the *Titanic* provided Bass Brewers with a unique and exclusive site for a tourist-like promotional event.

Bass associated itself with a televised expedition that attempted to raise a portion of the sunken wreck and also staked a proprietorial claim to a part of the ship's cargo—the 12,000 beer bottles that are believed to have gone down with the luxury liner. RMS Titanic Inc.—the firm that holds the salvaging rights to the ship—required Bass to rethink the nature of its promotion on a number of occasions. Thus, the grand prize winner of Bass's sweepstakes was not allow to descend to the wreck with a scientific crew in the submarine the *Nautile* because critics condemned such overt commercialization of the final resting place of so many people. Bass's U.S. importer, Guinness Import Corporation (GIC), instead offered ten contest winners the opportunity to sail to the expedition site on the luxury yacht *Ballymena*. Bass promoted the exclusive nature of the expedition, noting the $1,800 to $6,950 paid by the other two thousand expedition members, including celebrities such as Burt Reynolds, *Apollo II* astronaut Buzz Aldrin, and some survivors of the *Titanic*'s final voyage (Ringle 1996).

Although the attempt to raise a portion of the *Titanic* was one of the most unusual events ever used for commercial promotions and tie-ins, the Bass *Titanic* sweepstakes itself serves as a fairly standard example of contemporary multimedia and event marketing. Not surprisingly, the Bass sweepstakes and the RMS Titanic Inc. marketing of the cruise shared an interest in similar demographic and consumer profiles. For example, RMS Titanic ran conventional print advertisements in some of the largest daily newspapers in the United States and sent customized letters marked "URGENT" to residents in high-income zip codes, inviting recipients to "personally witness the first-ever raising of a major part [of the *Titanic*]" (Ringle 1996, B1, B8). For Bass and its U.S. importer, Guinness Import Corporation, however, the sweepstakes highlighted their product and simultaneously built a customized database from the demographic information they solicited from contestants. In addition to radio ads, the campaign also included point-of-purchase entry forms (which request name, address, age, and so on) and a Web site with its own demographic solicitations and contest entry forms ("Bass' Titanic Mission" 1996).

Bass's promotional event also benefitted from the Discovery Channel's documentation and subsequent telecast of the expedition. The cable channel's contribution of some $3 million toward the overall $5 million expedition budget saved the entire project—

and Bass's sweepstakes contest—from indefinite postponement. Members of the scientific community and the press—including some who had voiced concerns about the cruise—subsequently questioned the ethics of televising a mass burial site (Ringle 1996). And the bad press did not stop there. The event itself did not go as planned: some seventeen hundred onlookers—including Bass's contest winners—were forced to abandon their cruise after encountering bad weather. The attempt to raise a portion of the wreck likewise ended in failure after a series of technical glitches (Wilson-Smith 1996).

Thus, an event that had promised cutting-edge submersible technology in action, a live video transmission from the sunken wreck to a nearby celebrity-filled luxury yacht, a broadcast later on cable television, and salvaged cargo that would be put on display in exhibition halls across the United States and the world became ultimately a media spectacle. By including everyday Bass drinkers, consumers, and contest entrants, though, the expedition also publicized the underwater site, the contest promotion, and finally the product. In other words, the appeal of Bass's contest—within the overall marketing campaign—was based on the opportunity for a so-called average person to enter into the company of famous and wealthy people for a once-in-a-lifetime experience. The incorporation of such "elite" consumers in the promotion moreover highlights the contest's demographic (profiling) imperative within Bass's overall sales, advertising, and marketing plans.

Ironically, with all the potential ethical and political pitfalls that predetermined the staging of the event as a whole, the ultimate failure of the cruise and the salvage attempt at the site of the wreck contributed to the myth of the *Titanic* as a "persistent disaster" (Heyer 1995). The salvage failure meant the loss of potential exhibition fees for RMS Titanic Inc., but Bass's contest benefited from its association with the *Titanic*. By all accounts, Bass's *Titanic* promotion was such a success that the company revisited the same theme the following summer (1997). It ran a print advertisement in the *New York Times* (May 18, 1997, 25) that offered customers a mail-in cash-back coupon that required consumers to include an address, the universal product code (or bar code) from a purchased product, and a dated receipt, thus enabling Guinness Import Corporation to map its products, consumers, and points of sales. The advertisement also depicted a luxury steam line and a bottle of Bass Ale with the following invitation:

> Retrieving Bass Ale from the *Titanic* required lots of wet suits and shark repellent. Getting it home merely requires a passport. It's your chance to make history. Bass Ale invites you and a guest on a once-in-a-lifetime journey to England to return one of the bottles we've recovered from the legendary *Titanic*.

POLARPALOOZA 1995

> Molson USA requests that the general public refrain from any attempts to crash the party. We share in your enthusiasm for the event, but a personal journey to the Canadian Arctic would be unwise. It is indeed difficult it [sic] not impossible, to get to, and unfortunately, due to the lack of space in the small community of Tuktoyaktuk, Molson will not be able to accommodate anyone without a party invitation. You will have to win to get in.

Crashing a party has never seemed so hazardous. Trekking thousands of miles across the frozen tundra is clearly a dangerous endeavor, yet the above warning suggests that the American branch of the Canadian brewery Molson Inc. somehow felt it necessary—playfully or not[2]—to highlight this point when promoting its Polar Beach Party in 1995 (⟨http://www.molsonice.com⟩).

As was the case with Bass's *Titanic* promotion, Molson's Polar Beach Party—a rock concert featuring contemporary hard rock groups Hole, Metallica, Moist, and Veruca Salt—offered a unique spatial environment for the lucky winners of Molson's beer-cap and scratch-and-win contestants: three days on the Arctic Ocean in Tuktoyaktuk, Canada, some 200 miles north of the Arctic Circle.

The above warning is framed in the language of other music festivals. The request to "refrain from any attempts to crash the party," for example, sounds remarkably similar to the language used by promoters of Woodstock 1994 to avoid the gate crashing of the first Woodstock festival twenty-five years earlier. Similarly, the intimacy of a seemingly personalized "invitation" attempts to locate the event within the domesticity and distinct demographics of (largely male) North American teenage and college life. However, while the Arctic beach party was referred to in the musical and mainstream press as "Polarpalooza" (a reference to the multicity "alternative" or "modern rock" festival Lollapalooza), its location differentiated it from its contemporaries and predecessors. For example, the widespread consensus over the cultural and sociospatial meanings of the Woodstock concerts is that they were "outside" of or on the margins of mainstream American culture (as both a space and an event) and were heavily polluting events whose promoters publicly embraced an environmental-preservationist philosophy.

Beyond questions of territory and space, comparing the multiple corporate sponsorship of Woodstock 1994 (its 1969 predecessor was originally planned to promote a music recording studio planned for Woodstock, New York) with the single or exclusive sponsorship of the polar concert by Molson is difficult. Likewise, Bass's *Titanic* contest offers a useful case study of event marketing as a joint promotional venture that heightened product awareness, solicited demographics for GIC's marketing archives, and mediated the harsh, remote landscape and seascape, but the example of Molson's Polar Beach Party raises distinct symbolic and economic differences. Molson's decision to promote and produce the Polar Beach Party exclusively, for example, was a costly one, totaling some $10 million or twice the cost of the entire *Titanic* expedition. But the resulting unity of decision making and coordination of the event's overall production allowed Molson to exercise exclusive control over rights to the reproduction and broadcast of the event. Event participants differed also: the Bass event included scientific and celebrity participants, whereas the Molson Polar Beach Party invoked an authentic national landscape (the Canadian North, a frigid and potentially hazardous "extreme" Arctic environment) and an authentic human dimension (the Inuit people).

As Albert Nerenberg (1995) notes in his critical video of the event, entitled *Invasion of the Beer People*, the beach party was originally intended solely for Molson's American market but was later extended to Canada when the brewery realized the popularity of the promotion. That Canadian contestants were outnumbered by their American counterparts (approximately three to one), however, did not go unnoticed. In response to complaints in the Canadian press about "inviting more Yanks than Canadians," the *Boston Globe* clearly affirmed Molson's mythological campaign within the American psyche, reiterating Molson's promotional materials almost word for word: "There are more U.S. residents [participating in the event] because we're a larger country and a fertile market for Molson Ice, a style of nearly taste-free beer with a carefully developed image of being pure and strong." The *Globe* also quoted a Molson USA executive explaining that "Molson Ice became big in the United States because of the image that it was the beer from the land where ice was born" (Saunders 1995, 25). However, in spite of the Canadian national clichés (of wilderness, purity, ice, and snow) that seem to be etched in the American mind, the campaign's success also reaffirmed Canadians' own mythical thinking toward their environment, indigenous peoples of the North, and, in spite of the increased globalization of markets, Molson's loyalty to Canada's employment, economic, and cultural policy objectives.

THE CORPORATE EMBODIMENT OF CANADIAN CULTURE

As "North America's oldest brewery," Molson's association with Canadian culture dates back to the early administration of the colonial nation-state and the broadcasting of Canadian culture. Indeed, at the outset of his arrival in Montreal in 1782 from Britain, the brewery's founder, John Molson, set himself apart from the colony's principal fur trade institutions, the Hudson's Bay Company and North West Company. With a sound knowledge of farming techniques and grains, Molson quickly noted the absence of local breweries in the Montreal area, due in large part to the French inhabitants' preference for wine. The Molson dynasty was henceforth built on the separation of French and English consumer markets, an ironic beginning, given the ongoing separist sentiments in the Canadian federation (Woods 1983, 11). Always mindful of the political tensions between the Montreal's Anglophone business community and the French population, Molson nevertheless played a leading role in debates over the state of transportation in the territory. Recognizing the limits of sailing ships on the St. Lawrence River, the principal trade route between Montreal, Quebec City, and Europe, Molson set out to monopolize steam-powered shipping between the territory's main settlements. By 1811, however, Molson had failed to acquire such rights from Upper Canada's legislature (Woods 1983, 32–45).

Almost 150 years later, Molson again became a key player in nation-binding technologies. Responding to the corporate requirements for public relations and mass marketing Molson hired the Montreal Canadiens' hockey superstar Jean Beliveau in 1952 as a public relations representative. Beliveau's tenure was the beginning of a longstanding relationship between Molson's and hockey, Canada's unofficial national sport. Indeed, some five years later, in 1957, seeking a greater presence in Canadian culture, Molson bought the Montreal Canadiens and later used its new asset to procure the cosponsorship (with Imperial Oil) of the Canadian Broadcasting Corporation's nationwide telecast of *Hockey Night in Canada*, one of the nation's oldest broadcasts (Woods 1983, 297–299).

With the rise of free trade in the late 1980s, both interprovincially and internationally with the United States, Molson's protected market share and status as a Canadian institution was facing increased pressure from local cottage breweries, American breweries, and its chief Canadian rival, Labatt Brewing Company, owner of the Toronto Blue Jays, back-to-back baseball World Series winners. The competition became so intense that the introduction of "ice beer" into Canada in 1993 triggered an onslaught of legal battles between Molson and Labatt over both the rights to the label and the authenticity of the so-called ice-filtered brewing process. On similar grounds, legal wrangling later followed the introduction of "Molson Ice" into the American market, when Molson allied with the American conglomerate Philip Morris Companies and its subsidiary Miller Brewing Company. Even Australia's Carlton & United Breweries—which controls half of Molson Canada—suffered a similar fate when challenged by rival Australian Tooheys Brewing Co., which itself had introduced Hahn Ice (Martin 1993). This initial corporate posturing was therefore predicated not only on the ownership of the ice-filtered brewing process but also on its relationship with the space, weather, and nation of Canada (Berland 1993).

Within a year of releasing Molson Ice in the United States, a phalanx of ice beers flooded the market and by the middle of 1994
reached 5 percent of the U.S. beer market. Unlike the concept of
dry beer, which was imported from Japan, an American advertising
trade magazine noted with a degree of nationalist consternation
that "now that dry beers have gone flat, let's look north, to Canada" ("Dry Ice" 1994, 20). And in so doing, Anheuser-Busch
introduced Ice Draft, Miller released Lite Ice, Icehouse, Miller Ice,
and Miller High Life Ice, while Coors promoted its own Arctic
Ice. With the exception of Miller's Lite Ice and Anheuser-Busch's
Ice Draft, ice beers had a high alcohol content, so much so that in
February 1994 the U.S. Bureau of Alcohol, Tobacco, and Firearms
confirmed that it was investigating "the possibility [that] brewers
... or their distributors [were] illegally using alcohol strength
claims in marketing ice beers" ("Temperatures Rising on Ice Beer
Ads" 1994, 2). Even Miller Lite was advertised by the Chicago
advertising firm Leo Burnett within a "break-the-rules" theme.

Accompanying the phalanx of ice beers, Coors Lite was likewise promoted with images of snow-covered wilderness. During
breaks in sports programming, television commercials thus played a
hummable jingle ("Tap the Rockies ... Coors Lite") as a group of
giant twenty- and thirty-year-old men and women played football, dwarfing their ice-capped wilderness environment. At the
ad's conclusion, a giant young woman dwarfed a snow topped
ridge and slammed down a beer tap into the mountain range,
hence "Tapping the Rockies." The sounds and images of the
Coors Lite commercial are thus quite decipherable: the wintry,
rugged environment is a playground for the young; it is challenging yet refreshing, particularly when enhanced by an authentic
refreshment from its icy, natural essence. Furthermore, the participants by their very size attempt to conquer the wilderness through
ritualistic though rigorous play. Viewers we are thus taken to the
imaginary realm of the extreme.

Another iceless beer, Bud Lite, enters the ice phenomena with even greater significance for Canadian culture. As an official sponsor of the National Hockey League (NHL) in the United States, a sporting institution with historical roots on the ice rinks of Canada, Bud Lite becomes ice itself. Its logo is inscribed in paint underneath NHL ice rinks across the United States in plain view of the players, fans, and television viewing audience. Bud Lite therefore physically becomes part of the rituals of a sport's culture; it provides the grounding for the display of the sport's speed, power, and violence.

MOLSON POLAR BEACH PARTY

In an effort to distinguish itself from the many other brewers of ice beers, Molson conceived of a promotional event that would break into the male twenty-one to twenty-seven age bracket of the American market (Causey 1996). Preceding the Molson Ice Polar Beach Party in September 1995, Molson USA focused its advertisements on the slogan "Molson Ice, from the land where ice was born," a clear reference to both the home of the famous brewery and, with reminders of Molson's status as "North America's oldest brewery," to North American colonial history and settler sensibility. As was the case with the Coors Lite advertisement, Molson Ice coupled the actual "boldness" of the taste and excessive alcohol of the product with the cold and physically challenging Canadian landscape.

Not unexpectedly, then, Molson's "From the land where ice was born" print advertisements (Molson Breweries U.S.A. 1995, n.p.) added the following text, under the heading "Canada to the extreme":

> Each year thousands of thrill seekers assault the rugged mountainsides that fill Canada like ice cubes in a cup. Whether they are heli-skiers, snowborders, ice climbers, or

any other form of adrenaline junkie, Canada satisfies their
thirst for the extreme.

A relatively new phenomenon in televised sports culture, extreme
sports easily cross over from programming on the American cable
sports network ESPN to remarkably similar "music" programming
such as MTV sports. The first extravaganza of extreme sports, the
July 1995 *ESPN Extreme Games* broadcast, featured such daredevil
sports as street luge and sky surfing as well as other relatively
mainstream activities such as mountain biking. So successful was
the program that, according to *Newsweek* magazine (1995, 80), "it
sold six 'gold level' sponsorships to companies like Nike, Chevro-
let, and AT&T." Moreover, "a winter version may be next." Part
of the widespread appeal of such risk-taking, extreme leisure
activities seems to be the proximity of death or the unexplained.

Apart from extreme games (which were showcased on the Molson
Ice Web site), excessive alcohol, extreme cold, and remote space,
there remains the rock concert itself. The star of the Molson concert was Courtney Love, singer for the band Hole and widow of
the late rock icon Kurt Cobain. Not surprisingly, Love's persona as
an over-the-top excessive performer was a good match for the
event's focus on extremes. *The Globe and Mail* rightly noted in a
preview of the concert (Feschuk 1995a, A1) that "Nary a month
goes by in which [Love] ... does not find her way into the entertainment pages for passing out, throwing a fit, or trying to knock
someone's block off." As a result, the article proclaimed that Molson's Polar Beach Party's "Contest winners [will have to] brave
flurries, vendors, and Courtney Love's volatility." Love's arrival in
the Arctic hamlet of Tuktoyaktuk was, as a result, overdetermined
from the beginning (Feschuk 1995b, C3):

> Her face as white as the snow-capped peaks in those Molson
> Ice commercials, Courtney Love stepped through the door-
> way of the 737 and wobbled down its steps, seemingly

oblivious to the hoots of welcome from 50 or so Inuvialuit
kids. Safely reaching the ground despite bets to the contrary
from some onlookers, the singer ... was propped up by a
hunky female aide with pink hair, who also lit Love's ciga-
rette and helped keep the purse from slipping off Love's
arm.... A member of Hole's management later said that
Love was "disoriented."

If, as previously noted, the site of the concert differentiated it from
the history and conventions of other large concert events, then the
actual music and persona of the headline musicians further defined
its excessive theme. Moreover, the excessive sound, rhythm, and
lifestyle linked the concert event to the social space that was produced by the rugged landscape and various cultural appendages,
such as extreme sports. Clearly, a marketing campaign based on
"thrill seeking" would not be enhanced by a concert by Roger
Whittaker or by a concert performed at Toronto's Skydome.

INVITATIONS, SOLICITATIONS, AND MEDIATIONS

Although Molson's promotion invited a large targeted audience—
through print, radio, and TV ads—to participate in the contest,
the final five-hundred-person guest list for Molson's Polar Beach
Party was highly selective. In addition to the media, security, and
Molson's representatives, contest winners viewed the concert side
by side with Tuktoyaktuk's indigenous population. The inherently
contradictory nature of the event was evident in the town's
restrictions on alcohol sales. Since Tuktoyaktuk forbade the sale of
alcohol before the event and Molson wanted to take 13,000 cans
of beer to the event (averaging 26 beers per person), Molson
declared that it would not serve alcohol at the concert and that it
would give the town $20,000 outright and another $5,000 for
the local alcohol rehabilitation center. To help protect the

fragile Arctic environment, Molson "enlisted the help of an
American group, the Center for Marine Conservation" (〈http://
www.molsonice.com〉).

From beginning to end, then, the native people of Tuktoyaktuk
were omnipresent, giving a human face to the North. Accord-
ingly, the town's indigenous people perpetuated the "extreme" or
excess in authentic terms, forming a veritable "ethnoscape"
(Appadurai 1990) both in and surrounding the concert tent. Although the people of Tuktoyaktuk did not join the concert as an
equal partner, they "filled in" the geographical space with native
peoples, thus overdetermining the land's spatial boldness through
the insertion of—in southerners' eyes at least—those who seemingly successfully govern and overcome the excessive land, nature,
and weather of the Arctic.

Tuk's residents were invited to the event, adding to its authentic
aura, but their demographics and psychographics were not solicited. Conversely, Molson's contestants, successful or not, were
integrated into a much larger promotional enterprise—the reproduction of consumer markets. Whether on a rebate coupon, an
entry form, or a Web page, Molson integrated its market research
into a number of consumer practices. Consumers were urged,
for instance, to purchase specially marked boxes of Molson Ice
that were adorned with icebergs and the text "You could win
instantly." Consumers who found a "congratulations" sticker inside a box of Molson Ice beer were then required to forward their
name, address, and age to Molson. Likewise, the "second-chance
sweepstakes" required no purchase but asked consumers for their
name, address, and phone number.

Molson's exclusive control of the promotion of the event, moreover, meant that it also controlled the broadcasting rights to the
concert. In keeping with the spirit of the event and promotion as

a whole, the broadcasting (or narrowcasting) of the event was demographically exclusive. A ten-hour live Internet cybercast was broadcast through the Molson Ice Web page, and reception of the cybercast, which was hosted by an MTV V-jay, thus required a computer, high-speed Internet access, and knowledge of online software such as RealPlayer. Reception of the cybercast was also contingent on online membership at ⟨http://www.molsonice.com⟩. Not surprisingly, enrollment required answering a host of demographic questions (Booker 1995).

CONCLUSIONS

> There are great fjords and hot springs in Scandinavia, and those will be great images for our beer, but we don't want to give the impression that the beer is made out of hot springs that people are swimming in, so we're still working on the idea. Hot beer, the affjordable beer. (Gordon 1993, 9)

As we see in this parody of beer advertising, nationality often plays an integral part in marketing culture. In the Canadian case, we have seen the extent to which Labatt and Molson fought over what they, as it turned out, rightly believed to be a powerful international symbol—ice. In keeping with similar trends in the tourism industry, Molson thus framed its leisure- or travel-based marketing event as an exclusive and authentic once-in-a-lifetime event surrounded by alcohol, loud music, extreme sports, and the extreme and mythic environment of the Canadian Arctic. Juxtaposed against the tradition of the megaconcert and appropriately dubbed Polarpalooza, the Arctic concert offered a seemingly unattainable goal, that of "trekking"—albeit in a plane—to the North Pole, thus perpetuating the thrill of mastering space, nature, and weather.

Through the many sites of solicitation, contest entrants and winners also played an active role in the shift toward target marketing

and advertising in increasingly segmented consumer markets. Consumers were enticed to offer personal information in exchange for
a chance to win a unique prize, and successful contestants also
assisted in the commercial advertisement of the product. And
while Molson's targeting of probable consumers sheds light on
a company's active incorporation of personal information and
persons into a marketing apparatus, such beer drinkers and consumers do not appear to have been actively "disciplined" or otherwise subject to the panoptic effects discussed earlier in this book
(except perhaps through an increase in junk mail or other solicitations). The Inuit community (and its profile) was, conversely,
objectified to authenticate the purity of the "extreme" experience
and commodity.

As a relatively new and increasingly popular tactic, event marketing thus extends advertising appeals from the banal to the extreme,
from the everyday to the once in a lifetime, from the core to the
periphery (and back). The search for uncluttered commercial space
and time also calls into question the politics of using or *deploying*
profiles in promotional campaigns—in this case, the probable
consumer within a promotional event (highlighting national tensions) and the Inuits (and their immediate environment), who do
not fit the targeted profile but nonetheless assist in the process of
reproducing the market for Molson.

6

I initially disagreed with Arie Altena's (1999) claim that the Web browser had outlived its usefulness. If the browser was dead, as Altena claimed, then why was a corporation like America Online so interested in acquiring Netscape? Why would the U.S. federal government, in conjunction with many state governments, spend so much money trying to eliminate the monopolistic aspects of Microsoft's tactics in the "browser wars"? Since almost every previously autonomous computer network or program has migrated to the Web, isn't the Web browser more powerful than ever?

But Altena was less interested in the consumer use of the Web and more concerned with the artistic and creative possibilities of

THE "STATE" OF A PANOPTIC MEDIUM

the underlying decentered architecture of the Internet. The flexibility of the Web had overloaded the "dinosoar"-like 4.0 browsers that had effectively become "unmanageable, too big to maneuver with ease" (Altena 1999). Mobile applications on hand-held computers, and with specialized software and open-source software such as Linux have started to chip away at the assumption of universality—a one-size-fits-all Web browser.

The overwhelming popularity of Napster and a host of other similar peer-to-peer networks has also proven that the limits of the browser can be discussed in decidedly mass consumer terms. As a computer program that harnessed the decentered architecture of the Internet, at least for a short time, Napster's file-sharing software successfully challenged the music recording industry's stranglehold on the ownership and distribution of popular music. No successful challenges have yet been made to the corporate ownership and distribution of users' personal information on the Web. Rather, as this chapter shows, the Web browser and its accompanying "cookies" have played central roles in automating, to varying degrees, the collection of Web users' personal information. Any attempts by a user to qualify or reject the software's use of cookies (and by extension the corporate sponsor's collection of a user's personal Web-browsing habits) effectively crashes some of the most popular interactive functions of the Web, exposing the conditions and requirements of new media interactivity. Thus, Web cookies have effectively produced a symbiotic, panoptic relationship at the interface of the browser and the Web, an intransigent "state" that remains in place despite a diligent user's best attempts to change a browser's cookie preferences.

Most privacy advocates and theorists of media surveillance have warned that ubiquitous collecting of personal information—especially the automatic, enticed, or outright coerced collection of personal information—can lead to increased amounts of junk mail, identity theft, insecure consumer databases, and "social sorting" (Lyon 2001), customized Web content that limits access to different political perspectives and consumer products (Sunstein 2001). Although privacy concerns continue to be documented and debated in policy circles, such effects of online surveillance and user profiling do not by themselves explain *how* the collection of personal information is enabled by new media technologies. Likewise, the focus on panoptic effects cannot explain why users do not simply "opt out" of solicitation for personal information.[1]

This chapter argues that the Web-browser medium has become inseparable from the process of user surveillance. At its most basic level, Web surveillance—the solicitation of personal information and the tracking of user behavior—is enabled by a continuous connection between Web surfers and servers. Unfortunately, privacy-conscious users who try to counter the potential effects of online surveillance require extensive software expertise and a great deal of time to find the privacy preferences, and ultimately, even after a great deal of work, they discover that changing the cookie preferences of their browsers ends up degrading many popular interactive functions on the Web.

Cybersemiotics, Links, and Index Machines

The introduction of the first Web browsers in 1994 and 1995 was a pivotal moment in establishing an intransigent panoptic state on the Web, but a subtle proprietorial architecture had previously been encoded into the Web's particular form of hypertext. As one of the Web's chief inventors, Tim Berners-Lee (1999), acknowledges, hypertext markup language (html) for the Web sought to maintain authorial and editorial control over Web content and the characteristics of the networking of Web documents themselves through the insertion of hyperlinks. However, although such practices are the norm today on the Web, early hypertext systems, particularly Ted Nelson's Xanadu system (1960), allowed any user to add, delete, modify, or edit text and hyperlinks. Nelson thus envisioned a hypertext program that enabled universal access and promoted a populist ideology, generalist knowledge, pluralist politics, and a consequent engagement with controversial and radical ideas.[2] At the center of Nelson's system was the hyperlink itself, typically a word or phrase that when chosen would *automatically* take the user to the referred document. In Nelson's vision, the hyperlink was perhaps the single unifying element of the medium of hypertext: it laid bare the very conditions and practices of computerized connectivity, thematic associations, lines of argument, and potential "paths" of reading that a user could follow.

As has been argued elsewhere, hyperlinks serve distinct indexical goals, suggesting—and indeed providing the means to make—associative connections (Elmer 1997a; Shields 2000). With the advent of graphical Web browsers (Netscape's Navigator and Microsoft's Explorer), the indexical characteristics of hyperlinks were given added prominence through the deployment of a graphic user interface (GUI)—in particular, the choice of an iconic index finger as the cursor that enables the activation of a hyperlink. Thus, once a user positions a cursor on a hyperlink, the cursor is transformed into an index finger, signifying not only the link (as a keyword, an image, or a phrase) but also the actualization of Web connectivity. Bennington (1994) refers to this indexical characteristic as the process of *designation*, or the enabling of a particular course of events—in this instance, the connection to another Web document or site. Web hyperlinks are therefore not merely a sign or metaphor, as semioticians like Charles Peirce conceive them. Rather as a *deictic* index, they actually enable the connectivity of the Web-as-index.

After such decentered gateways to interdocument connectivity, association, and networking (via hyperlinks) were redesigned and formatted by Tim Berners-Lee (1999) and others for the Web (as hypertext markup language), though, they still raised serious questions about usability. How can a decentered document system with theoretically multiple entry and exit points (hyperlinks) be made workable? How can such a system be structured to enable efficient storage, search, and cataloguing functions? In short, where might users effectively begin to search this electronic, networked system?

The browser, through its default, start-up Web page (typically a Netscape-AOL or Microsoft "portal"—in essence an online categorized index), attempted to provide a searchable and universal point of departure for Web browsers. The popularity of such portals is unchallenged: AOL, MSN, Yahoo!, and Terra-Lycos, continue to consistently rank in the top five most visited sites on the Web.[3] Yet as Introna and Nissenbaum (2000) remind us, such portals (or to be more precise, the databases that are offered for these search engines) encompass fewer than half of all the sites on the Web. Search engines and portals, in other words, do not provide access to everything on the Web but rely on a host of strategies to construct selective representations of the Web. In addition to asking users to submit their sites for registration (as Yahoo!, for instance, recommends), search engines such as Google rely on automated cataloguing agents or "spiders" to construct their databases. According to Netcarta Corporation (1996, 1), the main producer of Internet mapping technologies,

> Spiders—also known as intelligent, user, or Internet agents —are commonplace on the World Wide Web, and perform a variety of onerous tasks automatically so users can be more productive. The most common spiders simply roam and mine the Internet for data.

Search engines like Google are not constructed by simply following hyperlinks from document to document (or from Web page to Web page). They also confer relevance and authority to Web sites based on the number of incoming links. Sites with more links, in other words, are more apt to rate highly on Google's lists of search "hits." The Google database thus constructs a hierarchical metaindex from a topography of hyperlinks. With the help of the browser, the search engine—as a database of Web pages and sites—renders an indexical form of Web connectivity. As a consequence, Web sites and pages are no longer atomized or decentralized.

Surveillance on the Web is a similar means of sorting and categorizing users and is enabled by a similar logic of connectivity, not unlike how hyperlinks connect documents. Web surveillance is largely concerned with facilitating reliable and continuous *connections* between users and (largely) commercial servers. In fact, one might argue that on the seemingly discontinuous Net, making connections (and keeping them) have become the primary commercial strategy. Continuous computer-mediated communication via instant messaging programs, for example, has become a hotly competitive technology that Microsoft, Yahoo!, and America Online have used to acquire new subscribers, users, and consumers.

E-tailers and other consumer-driven online Web sites initially viewed Internet users as a decidedly disconnected class and made periodic requests to large servers for content, services, and commodities. In Internet parlance, users and e-tailers were mired in a "stateless" environment, with no overarching mechanism for continuous, two-way interaction. With the advent of the first Netscape browsers, however, the Internet became both increasingly more visual and decidedly more connected, especially between individual users and Web site proprietors. Netscape's cookies provided Web sites and servers with continuous and often automatic access to users' hyperlinked browses. They also challenged users' exclusively *personal* use of their personal computers. The PC hard drive has become for most purposes the end node of the Net—the point at which personal information is continuously integrated into the medium of the Web.

TRACING THE COOKIE TRAIL

Cookies have become one of the primary means of identifying individuals on the Web (particularly for e-tailers) and as such have become the source of much concern for privacy advocates worldwide. This chapter examines the relationship between Internet software (specifically Web browsers and their accompanying cookies) and the privacy rights of online users (defined as the desire to maintain control over the dissemination of personal demographic and psychographic information). The chapter discusses a research study that I made of Netscape's Navigator and Communicator Web browsers—specifically, versions 1.12 (1995), 2.02, 3.0 (1996), 4.01, and 6.01 (2000)—and that asked where browsers locate preferences for cookies, cookie files, and information about cookies and which options they offered for controlling the use of cookies. As a whole, this study looked at user knowledge and control over cookie operations via the Web browser and the PC hard drive. Its questions attempt to ascertain the degree to which Netscape encodes knowledge and control preferences for Web browser cookies. Findings from a brief follow-up study also shed light on the implications of having users actually change the default settings[4] of their cookie operations (when available). In short, both studies suggest that Internet users who exert their privacy rights in cyberspace by disabling their browser's cookie preferences also significantly disable the Web's ability to offer them convenient services and relevant information (in particular, information offered by industry leaders such as Yahoo! and Excite).

COOKIES: CULTIVATING THE ONLINE CONSUMER STATE

When a user visits a Web site, the site sends a small identifying piece of information, or "cookie," to a personal computer within a hypertext transfer protocol (HTTP) header. When users stop to view certain Web sites and pages, therefore, they receive text, graphics, streaming media, and so forth on their screens, but they also receive a small packet of information that is stored in the browser's memory and then stored on their own hard drives when the browser is closed (Whalen 2001). Privacy expert Roger A. Clarke (2001) offers a clear step-by-step explanation:

- A Web browser requests a page from a Web server;

- The Web server sends back to the Web browser not just the requested page but also an instruction to the browser to write a cookie (i.e., a record) into the client-computer's storage;

- Unless something prevents it, the Web-browser does so;

- Each time a user requests a Web page, the Web browser checks whether a cookie exists that the Web server expects to be sent with the request . . . ;

- If there is such a cookie, the browser transmits the record to the Web server, along with the request for the page;

- When a Web server receives a request that has a cookie associated with it, the server is able to use the data in the cookie in order to "remember" something about the user.

The purpose of employing cookies, in the technical language of the Net, is to overcome a "stateless protocol" (Whalen 2001). Simply put, cookies provide a relatively stable platform for interactions between users (clients) and Web site owners (or servers). Cookies essentially provide servers (and their owners) a means of identifying repeat visitors to their Web sites, and in so doing they fundamentally challenge the ability of users to remain anonymous on the Net.[5] Thus, in addition to offering the possibility of online user surveillance, early cookie technology also provided ease of use and personalized information sources. Approximately eighteen months after the technology was first introduced in December 1994, cookies were being used for three main purposes—retaining information at e-tailing sites (such as items placed in online "shopping baskets"), personalizing content on Web sites, and providing Web owners (or "masters") with information on how users are navigating their respective Web sites (Randall 1997).

Despite these seemingly obvious benefits to online consumers, Netscape and later Microsoft (Internet Explorer) neglected to make public the use of cookie technology in 1995 and early 1996.[6] In hindsight, such a declaration might have diffused some early criticism and ongoing distrust of cookie technology. The first published reports of cookie technology were certainly a public relations challenge for Netscape. Not surprisingly, the specter of an Orwellian World Wide Web was repeatedly raised by reporters and other critics of Netscape. One of the earliest newspaper articles on cookies, published in the *Financial Times*, for example, exclaimed that "Technology is already in place—and ready to be put to use on the World Wide Web of the Internet—that will allow Web site owners to gather an alarming range of information on the people who look at their Web pages from PCs at home" (Jackson 1996, 15).

Defenders of such technology argue that cookies transmit only a few pieces of information to Web page owners and e-tailers— namely, the user's Internet Protocol (IP) address,[7] the type of Web browser, and the operating system of the personal computer (U.S. Department of Energy 1998). However, as the following discussion of cookie control preferences demonstrates, the relatively small amount of information transmitted by cookies was greatly enhanced when Web site operators linked that information with server data-collection and -diagnosis techniques (most prominently user profiling, collaborative filtering, and recommender systems). As cookies were used more widely by clients (users) and servers (largely e-tailers but also government),[8] Netscape began to release new versions of its popular browser that provided additional information and options for controlling the use of cookies. Netscape's changes highlight the growing importance of Web "literacy" and also the effects of choosing Netscape's own cookie-control preferences (namely, the disruption and disabling of Web convenience and relevance).

Table 6.1

Comparison of Cookie Features in Netscape 1.12, 2.02, 3.0, 4.01, and 6.01

Netscape Version (for Macintosh)	Preferences Location	Privacy Control Options
1.12 (August 1995)	None	None
2.02 (May 1996)	None	None
3.0 (August 1996)	Options, Network preferences, Protocols	Show an Alert before Accepting a Cookie, Default setting: Off
4.01 (June 1997)	Edit, Preferences, Category: Advanced	Accept all cookies, Accept only cookies that get sent back to the originating server, Do not accept cookies, Warn me before accepting a cookie, Default setting: Accept all cookies
6.01 (February 2001)	Tasks, Privacy and security, Cookie manager *Other option:* Edit menu, Preferences, Advanced	Enable all cookies, Enable cookies for the originating Web site only, Disable cookies, Warn me before storing a cookie, View stored cookies, Allow cookies from this site, Block cookies from this Site, Remove Cookie, Remove all Cookies, Don't allow removed cookies to be accepted later, Default setting: Enable all cookies

THE EVOLUTION AND DEVOLUTION OF COOKIE PREFERENCES: A VERSION-BY-VERSION ANALYSIS

Five versions of Netscape's browser were studied (table 6.1, column 1). Although the study focused on Netscape's browser on a Macintosh platform or operating system, few significant variations or options were observed in other platforms (Netscape for Windows and Microsoft's competing Internet Explorer browser),[9] though an examination of Microsoft's bundling and use of Net-

Cookie Files Location	Information on Cookies
System folder, Preferences folder, Netscape folder, Magic cookie file	None
System folder, Preferences folder, Netscape folder, Magic cookie file	None
System folder, Preferences folder, Netscape folder, Magic cookie file	Preference panels guide, *Netscape Navigator Handbook*
Netscape Communicator folder, Communication, User name folder, Magic cookie file	Help, Advanced panel
Mozilla folder, Users50, Default folder, Mgb93svy.slt folder, Cookies file	Help, Understanding privacy, Also, "More information" tab in the cookie preference section leads to the understanding privacy document.

scape with a Microsoft Windows 98 operating system would require a full chapter. Netscape has released forty-one browser versions (not including beta versions), but the study focused on only versions that made substantive changes (defined as either information or control/alert options) to cookie preferences.

The second column in table 6.1, Preferences Location, relates to the place in the respective version of Netscape's browser, typically pull-down menus, where users can find and change the preferences for cookies. *Preferences* is the term widely used in the computer software industry to refer to the options that users are given to change various software functions. Many software programs, including Netscape for Macintosh, use the label Preferences for their pull-down menus. The Preferences pull-down menu for Netscape offers a daunting list of potential options, ranging from appearance options (including fonts), network proxies, cache, and, of course, cookies. Such software preferences or control options serve as a key indicator of a software's flexibility and usability. There is no one established list of options or preferences for all software. Some software programs provide few options for customization and adaptation to computing requirements. Other programs offer a lengthy and exceedingly complex list of options, some of which pose potential systemwide hazards in the hands of all but the most computer-literate users.

Preferences and similar control options thus shed light on the limits of software and the choices that are made in the process of producing software. And although software programmers make decisions so that their company's software will be compatible and complementary to their company's other products or an allied corporation's software, other preference decisions are often made for reasons of cost, time, efficiency, or simply ignorance of other possible options and can result in the shelving of more dynamic plans.[10]

Production decisions—made by computer programmers and software industry executives—have clear social, political, ethical, and of course economic implications.[11] Seen in this light, the default settings of various preferences that are set at the factory assume a lowest-common-denominator software user and suggest a "recommended" or preferable mode of use (for the benefit of the user, the software developer, and the developer's corporate allies). The sections on the five browser versions provide more on these points.

The third column in table 6.1—Privacy Control Options—lists the actual preferences. These boxes, circles, and other interactive buttons let users change the function of cookies. In addition to providing their location and default setting, the terminology used for such options also provides some insight into Netscape's attempts to respond to social criticism of cookie technology.

The fourth column—Cookie Files Location—lists the storage area for cookies after a user has visited a Web site. The complicated locations call into question the accessibility of cookie files, their appearance (are they presented in plain language, expert PC vernacular, or computer code?), and the very preferences for the files themselves (can they be edited, deleted, renamed, or color-coded like text, graphics, or html files?).

The last column—Information on Cookies—attempts to show the extent to which each version provides documentation on the workings of cookie technology. Almost all computer software and programs today are accompanied by either a "read-me.txt" or "text" file or for more advanced products an online Help index or frequently asked questions (FAQ) section.

Versions 1.12 and 2.02

Netscape's earliest browser versions are completely devoid of any preferences, control options, or information on cookies. Cookies were operational in all version 1 (1995) and version 2 (May 1996) browsers, but users were not able to manipulate their workings and were not even aware of their existence. Because the first version of Netscape had no preferences or options for controlling the use of cookies, by default it accepted all cookie files that were sent back by Web sites. Subsequently, the new cookie-enabled Internet (as a networking of computers) meant that personal computers and their accompanying hard drives were no longer personal.

The only evidence of cookies in versions 1 and 2 is the Magic Cookie File (see the column headed Cookie Files Location). There is no clear path to this file or any information that suggests its existence or greater significance for the individual user. The file itself is a simple generated text file that cannot be edited in any manner. Even a lengthy reading of the *Netscape Handbook* (version 1), with its tutorial, reference guide, and index, reveals no mention of cookies or client-server states at all. In fact, the "Filling in [online] Forms" section of the "Learn Netscape" portion of the *Handbook* is the most obvious and applicable place to mention cookie technology, given that such online forms employ cookies to "remember" repeat visitors. The section, however, merely offers the following passage about the convenience of the Web browser (Netscape 1995):

> Typically, forms are used to give you a fast and easy way to make a request or send back a response regarding the page you are reading. Forms can supply an interface to databases with fields that let you query for information and perform Internet searches.

Version 3.0

The earliest discussions of cookie technology were published in newspapers and popular technology periodicals just prior to the release of the Netscape 2.02 browser, so it shows no evidence of substantive changes from version 1.12. However, as concern over cookies mounted in spring 1996, news reports indicated that Netscape would offer options for cookie use in its upcoming version 3.0 (August 1996) (Rigdon 1996). Table 6.1 shows that the preferences for cookies (control options) were obscurely labeled (Options, Network Preferences, Protocols) and did not mention "cookies" or other common language such as "privacy or identity controls." Without substantial knowledge of cookies or computer language, users could not easily recognize or find the cookie preference. Although the Magic Cookie File remained in the same place as it had in previous versions, information on cookies was added to an expanded *Netscape Handbook 3.0*. Given the many criticisms of Netscape's treatment of privacy control options, the *Handbook* offered very little that explained cookie technology. Indeed, as with earlier handbooks, discussions of client-server interactions (the raison d'être of cookie technology) lack any reference to cookies (Netscape 1996):

> The server transmits page information to your screen. The Netscape application displays the information and leaves the connection to the server open. With an open connection, the server can continue to push updated pages for your screen to display on an ongoing basis.

Indeed, of all the information provided by Netscape (including a cookieless eighteen-page document that lists "What's New Since 2.0?"), the new cookie preference receives almost the briefest description (Netscape 1996):

> The Alert check Boxes determine whether you receive a notification dialog box (popup alert) when accepting a cookie (unchecked, by default) or submitting a form by mail. (A cookie is a piece of limited, internal information transmitted between server software and the Netscape application.) The dialogs notify you before information is transmitted.

The most significant and relevant change to version 3.0 was the option Show an Alert before Accepting a Cookie. If a user changes the preference from the default No position (do not alert) and visits a cookie-enabled Web site, a notification appears in a box asking the user, "Do you wish to allow the cookie to be set?" Buttons with the options No and Yes are provided. The Yes option is set as a default, meaning that a user who simply hits Return is choosing the Yes option (allow cookies).

Moreover, such seemingly minor changes to the Netscape browser hint at the political debate over privacy and anonymity online and also point to the broadening use of cookie technology throughout the burgeoning Internet industry. To unearth the expansion of cookie technology, I visited a representative sample of Web sites that included two search engines (MyExcite and MyYahoo!), a content provider (NYTimes.com), and an e-commerce provider (Yahoo! shopping) using the new cookie alert option for the 3.0 browser (table 6.2). After the alert was received, both options—do not accept the cookie and accept the cookie—were tested. Although the Netscape browser allowed users to control the storage of cookies on their hard drives, choosing to decline cookies blocked access to the aforementioned sites. In other words, if a user wanted the convenience of reading the *New York Times*, shopping online at Yahoo!, or personalizing content at the Yahoo! or Excite Web sites, then they had to accept the cookie files.

Version 4.01

With users' concerns still mounting over cookies, in June 1997 Netscape released the 4.01 version of its browser (table 6.3).

Table 6.2
Netscape 3.0

Options	NYTimes.com	MyYahoo!	Yahoo! Shopping	MyExcite.com
"Show an alert before accepting a cookie." • No (cookie is not set) • Yes (cookie is accepted)	• In order to access NYTimes.com, your Web browser must accept cookies. • Access allowed	• An error occurred setting your user cookie. • Access allowed	• Sorry! You must configure your browser to accept cookies in order to shop at this merchant. • Access allowed	• Please enable your browser to accept cookies. • Access allowed

Cookie control functions were no easier to find, nor did they particularly encourage novice users to experiment with the cookie-control functions. The preferences panel now simply offered cookie controls under the daunting title Advanced (see table 6.1). The browser offered four options—accept, decline, warn before accepting a cookie, and accept "only cookies that get sent back to the originating server." The fourth choice was a response to the news that third parties, originally hackers, were able to "read" cookies left behind by a host of Web sites and offer the raw materials for a personal profile of the user (based on the history of sites visited by the user).

Initially, cookies were meant to bridge an individual user's computer to a single server, such as a respective e-tailer like Amazon.com or CDNow.com. But individual hackers were not

Table 6.3

Netscape 4.01

Options	NYTimes.com	MyYahoo!	Yahoo! Shopping	MyExcite.com
A. Accept only cookies that get sent back to the originating server.	Access allowed	Access allowed	Access allowed	Access allowed
B. Do not accept cookies.	In order to access NYTimes.com, your Web browser must accept cookies.	An error occurred setting your user cookie.	Sorry! You must configure your browser to accept cookies in order to shop at this merchant.	Please enable your browser to accept cookies.
C. Warn me before accepting a cookie. • Cancel (cookie is not set) • OK (cookie is accepted)	• In order to access NYTimes.com, your Web browse must accept cookies. • Access allowed	• An error occurred setting your user cookie. • Access allowed	• Sorry! You must configure your browser to accept cookies in order to shop at this merchant. • Access allowed	• Please enable your browser to accept cookies. • Access allowed

the only ones trying to bypass this one-to-one cookie setting. The online advertising giant Doubleclick, for instance, partnered with a number of online Web sites to set individual server-addressed cookies from multiple remote sites. Visiting a page from a Doubleclick partner, regardless of its URL (Web address), thus resulted in the storage of a Doubleclick cookie. Doubleclick used the information collected at these partnered sites to target specific and "relevant" commercial messages to individual users. Responding to criticism of such online profiling, Doubleclick later offered an "opt-out" option through its Web site. Ironically, opting out was contingent on accepting a cookie from Doubleclick.

Version 6.01

After Netscape was taken over by Internet service provider giant America Online (AOL), its browsers took a decidedly different approach to cookies, especially in its accompanying help material.

Table 6.4

Netscape 6.01

Options	NYTimes.com	MyYahoo!	Yahoo! Shopping	MyExcite.com
A. Enable cookies for the originating Web site only.	Access allowed	Access allowed	Access allowed	Access allowed
B. Disable cookies.	In order to access NYTimes.com, your Web browse must accept cookies.	An error occurred setting your user cookie.	Sorry! You must configure your browser to accept cookies in order to shop at this merchant.	Please enable your browser to accept cookies.
C. Warn me before storing a cookie. • No (cookie is not set) • Yes (cookie is accepted)	• In order to access NYTimes.com, your Web browser must accept cookies. • Access allowed	• An error occurred setting your user cookie. • Access allowed	• Sorry! You must configure your browser to accept cookies in order to shop at this merchant. • Access allowed	• Please enable your browser to accept cookies. • Access allowed

Netscape 6 (2001) and its updates provide comprehensive documentation on cookies (table 6.4). The Privacy document contains over five pages on cookies and more pages on online privacy issues in general. Netscape's documentation now points its finger at rogue Web sites and other interests less concerned about privacy. In the section that asks "Why Reject Cookies?" Netscape's privacy documentation (Netscape 2000) now reads:

> If a site can store a cookie, it can keep track of everything you've done while visiting the site by writing these things into a cookie that it keeps updating. In this way, it can build a profile on you. This may be a good or a bad thing depending on what the site does with the information.... It might be bad if the bookseller then sold that information to the local dog pound so they could cross-check for potential dog owners who do not have valid dog licenses.

Netscape's attempts to share the blame for cookie abuse has not resulted in any radical modifications in the way cookies are encoded into browser preferences. The default setting is not "Do not accept cookies," and new and intermediate users still have to dig deep into the program to find out about privacy and cookie controls. Part of the reason for this lack of modification is that the Web would become a much less convenient and relevant place if it had generic "lowest common denominator" portals, offered leaky online shopping bags, and showed advertisements for products and services that the user had never previously bought or browsed. Moreover, such inconvenience would disproportionately fall on Netscape and its Web browser—especially when Web sites such as Yahoo! remark (if a user visits with cookies turned off) that "The browser you're using refuses to sign in. (cookies rejected)."

Having a cookie warning set as the default choice would be even more maddening, although it is potentially the most instructive

way to demonstrate the extent to which cookie technology is used
on the Web. A browse through Amazon.com, for instance, with
the "Warn me before accepting a cookie" option chosen results in
multiple interruptions to show the message "The site amazon.com
wants to set a cookie. Do you want to allow it?" Being asked for a
cookie preference on multiple pages within a site would be very
inconvenient. A user could not knowledgeably discriminate between one Web site cookie and another, particularly when bom-
barded with requests from page to page. The cookie manager in
Netscape version 6.0 follows a similar logic by offering the option
of deleting individual cookies but providing little to no help in
distinguishing one cookie file from another (except perhaps a
warning about the aforementioned "foreign cookies" employed by
advertising brokers such as Doubleclick).

Conclusions

Technological periodicals, academics, and newspaper articles routinely define cookies as "a few lines of text," "short pieces of
information," "a record," or simply "a number." Ironically, Netscape is one of the few sources that accurately define cookies as
"a mechanism." In the more widely circulated "data" definition,
we find a consistent client (user) definition after the fact—that is,
absent the process by which such pieces of "data" come to be
stored on or accessed via a user's hard drive. And although Netscape's definition correctly focuses on the technology and not on
the product of the technology, the company's actual deployment
of cookies since 1994 has a much closer affinity with the "data"
definition. In other words, the Netscape browser's privacy solu-
tions or controls for cookies focus on the cookie files on users'
own hard drives.

As this chapter has shown, the act of disabling cookies highlights
their link to the server side of the Web where once convenient

and relevant sites such as MyYahoo! now inform users that their decision to refuse cookies has produced an "error." With the help of a default set on "Accept cookie" preferences and cookie options that significantly limit, disable, or disrupt the convenient flow of relevant online information and services, the release of personal online information (previously automated in early versions of Netscape browsers) has now become either an automatic or forced "choice" for PC Web users.[12] Debate continues about the effects of panoptic surveillance, but new media such as the Web, which make content more relevant and easier to consume, increasingly construct an intransigent panoptic state within the very functioning of the medium.

7

A profile ... is a kind of prior ordering, ... a model or figure that organizes multiple sources of information to scan for matching or exceptional cases. Resembling an informated form of stereotyping, profiling technology has become increasingly popular in targeting individuals for specialized messages, instructions, inspection, or treatment. Advertisers use it to determine the timing and placement of ads to reach the widest segment of selected audiences. Educators use it to adjust course content to specific populations of students, police to target potential offenders. Profiling, in turn, is only one of a host of increasingly available computer-assisted actuarial and diagnostic procedures that are being used,

THE POLITICS OF PROFILING

among other things, to identify individuals for various tasks and or entitlements, to define potential risks or hazards, and to forestall or enhance certain behaviors and traits. Unlike stereotypes, however, profiles are not merely "false images" that are used to justify differences in power. Diagnostic profiles exist rather at the intersection of actual and virtual worlds. (Bogard 1996, 27)

Interest in profiling is at an all-time high in the United States—in films, in books, and on television news programs,[1] but the practice remains surprisingly abstract. Although profiling maintains a certain enigmatic quality, it does have specific applications, technologies, and spaces—all elements that I touch on to varying degrees in this book. In this final chapter, I discuss the conceptual framework of consumer profiling and its place within previous cultural studies of technology, media, and consumption, particularly as it applies to politics.

William Bogard's *The Simulation of Surveillance: Hypercontrol in Telematic Societies* (1996) is one of the few sustained critiques of the technology and politics of profiling, but I believe that a relatively simple logic is behind the need to construct a picture out of the seemingly infinite qualities of everyday life. To profile is to attempt to account for the unknown—our inability to adequately capture, contain, or regulate and govern behavior, thought, language, and action. In a recent article (Elmer 1997b), I note the proliferation of television shows that feature profiling (most prominently NBC's *Profiler* and Fox's *The X-Files* and *Millennium*) and the inability of their characters to capture the criminal, to know what's "out there," or in fact to know who is even human. To combat this precarious state of affairs, the protagonists in these programs and other shows and films that feature law enforcement[2] try to match patterns of criminal (or alien) behavior to the *modus operandi* (MOs) of known (meaning catalogued) criminals. The one-size-fits-all profile typically describes a male in his late thirties who is a loner with above-average intelligence.

Such contemporary narratives, stories, plots, and programming all play on the link between the widespread fear of the unknown and the need to profile—to come up with at least some picture of the transgressor. Not surprisingly, social fears of the unknown were also heightened throughout the year 1999 by uncertainties over how computers would react on December 31. The apocalypse that might be triggered by the new millennium was not a moral disaster but a technological crisis for information networks. What the new millennium therefore potentially brings is a systematic, automated corruption of the networks of information—bugs, viruses, and outdated chips that can disable the simplest tasks of everyday life.

Although this book has focused on the complex technological elements of profiling within our consumer culture, the fields of criminology and psychology have also provided insights into its discriminatory applications. The historian and novelist Caleb Carr, for instance, offers a compelling look at an early use of criminal profiling through a mix of narrative fiction and historical fact. Set in New York City in 1896, Caleb's *The Alienist* (1994) opens with a detailed description of a series of unimaginably gruesome murders. At first it appears that the authorities have failed to recognize the relationship or pattern among similar crimes perpetrated over a period of two years. Later, however, readers learn that the police department's lack of interest in the crimes was in no small part due to the nature of the victims, who are all teenage male prostitutes. The crimes are invisible to the public eye, and the book's chief protagonist, a crime reporter for the *New York Times*, notes that his editors view stories about such crimes as unfit to print. The book's first chapters also introduce the members of what becomes the city's "unofficial" investigations unit—the crime reporter, two marginalized Jewish New York City police detectives, and Dr. Laszlo Kreizler, an enigmatic psychologist (or "alienist").[3]

In *The Alienist*, Carr provides a lavish description of the moral landscape of late nineteenth-century Manhattan as well as a discussion of the social implications of the convergence of mathematical statistics (specifically, the establishment and significance of patterns) with behavioral psychology. Consequently, his main characters are developed largely through their relationships to the production and utility of simulated pictures of probable social, political, and criminal transgressors. Thus, whereas academic authors such as Ian Hacking (1990) and Armand Mattelart (1996) offer compelling discussions of the relationship between statistics, measurements, and the governance of the nation-state, Carr's piece of fiction sheds light on the social and political dimensions of tracking, profiling, and hence governing *individual* behavior. As Carr's most engaging character, Dr. Kreizler, notes (Carr 1994, 61):

> We know nothing of the person we seek, and are unlikely ever to find witnesses who know more than we do. Circumstantial evidence will be sparse at best—he has been at work for years, after all, and has had more than enough time to perfect his technique. What we must do—the only thing that *can* be done—is to paint an imaginary picture of the sort of person that *might* commit such acts. If we had such a picture, the significance of what little evidence we collected would be dramatically magnified. We might reduce the haystack in which our needle hides to something more like a—a pile of straw, if you will.

One of the politically questionable results of this shift in tactics—from attempting to track the actions of individual criminals to researching the qualities of possible or probable transgressors through patterns of behavior—is the production of broadly defined "deviant" social profiles (such as the aforementioned white male loner as the quintessential one-size-fits-all criminal profile). When such broad and all-encompassing descriptions are produced, profiling *virtually* (literally and figuratively speaking) "guarantees" and "serves up" a phalanx of typically marginalized individuals for surveillance (Bogard 1996, 28). Given that such profiles are embedded with cultural and social values, alongside or in spite of the hard evidence or clues in any one case, potential discriminatory applications are all too apparent. "Driving while black" is the best-known and most widely reported misuse of racial profiling on highways by law enforcement.[4] The race-based traffic stop is an example of excessively broad (indeed, biopolitical) profiling in which African Americans and Latinos are stopped and interrogated by authorities merely because of their race and ethnicity. Racial profiling, then, moves beyond individual acts of prejudice and racism by law enforcement officers to the realm of institutional policy. The power of racial profiling lies not so much in its "representational" status, for example, as stereotypes, but rather as blueprints—or diagrams—that actively serve to discriminate populations in search of possible transgressors.

PROFILES AS REPRESENTATIONS

In many respects, this book has attempted to provide a model of analysis of the fears and uncertainties that profiling techniques and technologies are attempting to address. An implicit theme in many if not all of the previous chapters has been the questioning of strictly visual critiques of consumer culture. Within the burgeoning field of cultural studies, particularly film and television studies, semiotic models of analysis have successfully demonstrated the arbitrariness of the sign (Barthes 1957, 126) and subsequently the ideological and cultural aspects of communication, particularly mass-mediated imagery.[5] Attempts to contextualize the ocular dimension of consumption have also played a pivotal role in debates over the ideological nature of the media.

In so doing, influential frameworks—such as Stuart Hall's encoding and decoding model (1980), which assesses the sphere of production and also the ways in which audiences watch, consume, and make meaning out of cultural programming—have also highlighted a number of limitations. First, although some have successfully contextualized the consumption of media texts in the domestic sphere (Morley 1986; Lull 1990), these spaces of consumption remain relatively static and unproblematized, not altogether unlike Foucault's panoptic subjects.[6] Second, the semiotic and encoding/decoding models have been overwhelmingly restricted to the consumption of televisual texts. Consumption and production in databases and on the Internet remain uncharted. Finally, such a focus on watching has restricted "representation" to the film or videotape frame. What is missing from the frame becomes underrepresented. Distortions become "misrepresentations." Within Hall's model, these strictly textual definitions have given rise to a series of protracted debates pitting theories of mass culture against theories of popular culture. The so-called resistance debate, drawn from John Fiske's (1989a, 1989b, 1992) reading of Michel de Certeau's *The Practice of Everyday Life* (1984), is perhaps the inevitable result of a dichotomous model that produces either duped or resistive audiences. Although television certainly retains and even expands its cultural power, this book questions the implications of the forms of consumption that take place in an almost infinite number of places, at varying times of the day and night, and through an increasingly complex network of communication, information, and consumer technologies.

Technological, topographical, and theoretical (particularly post-structuralist) problematics, however, have led to a rethinking of methodological and analytical questions within the fields of media and cultural studies. The Culture, Media, and Identities series of books written or edited by Paul du Gay, Stuart Hall, and others from the Open University in the United Kingdom, for example (Sage Publications, 1997–2001), has attempted to broaden the scope of cultural methodologies and the binary producer-consumer model. Du Gay's series introduction is clearly influenced by Richard Johnson's (1986) questions on the analysis of culture and is quite illustrative in this regard (du Gay 1997, 3–4):

> The five major cultural processes which the book identifies are *Representation, Identity, Production, Consumption,* and *Regulation....* Taken together, they complete a sort of circuit—

what we term the circuit of culture—through which any analysis of a cultural text or artifact must pass if it is to be adequately studied.... Remember that this is a circuit. It does not much matter where on the circuit you start, as you have to go the whole way round before your study is complete. What is more, each part of the circuit is taken up and reappears in the next part, that is, of how *Identities* are constructed. And so on. We have separated these parts of the circuit into distinct sections, but in the real world they continually overlap and intertwine in complex and contingent ways.

Each of the five categories within du Gay's "circuit of culture" may or may not be restricted to the study of mere "artifacts" and "texts," but the model affords a flexible, almost cybernetic system of reproduction. The authors describe this approach as a "third way" that considers people "in action" (du Gay et al. 1997, 102). What remains sketchy in Hall and du Gay's analytical model, however, is its treatment of the political, which is somewhat surprising given the aforementioned debate over political action and resistance in cultural studies. *Doing Cultural Studies: The Story of the Sony Walkman*, the book that sets the tone and philosophy of the entire book series (du Gay, Hall, Janes, Mackay & Negus 1997), unfortunately remains largely descriptive as it follows a commodity through the five interconnected "stages" of the circuit. In the book's conclusion, the authors mention the manner in which the commodity in question (the Sony Walkman) coincides with and to some degree facilitates the privatization of public space (du Gay et al. 1997, 120). On the question of politics, such a model probably would emphasize the importance of democracy and space.

Unlike the "circuit of culture" model, my arguments in this book have emphasized the *place* and role of the individual within the broad technological system of cultural and economic reproduction. In so doing, I have offered a similar circular methodology—a "diagrammatic method" that can account for commodities as well as the accumulation, diagnosis, and mapping of personal information, all pivotal elements in the ongoing reproduction of consumer markets. In other words, as consumers, citizens, parents, children, members of various ethnic groups, and so on we are represented (or misrepresented) in and through texts, and we are actively solicited for our opinions, likes, wants, and desires in the process of rationalizing and revising various elements of sales, distribution, advertising, and marketing. Before we move to any understanding of politics, we therefore must first understand the terms on which a system reproduces itself—the techniques that are employed to rationalize, map, and govern.

SPATIAL ROUTINES AND EVERYDAY HABITS

To locate potential sites of political struggle, we must determine the sites at which we enter or engage particular systems of power and discrimination, and for this reason, I have consistently returned to questions of space. Consumer culture is increasingly characterized by its ability to seep into every dimension of our lives so insidiously that the landscape and topography become veritable billboards and potential sites of consumer "feedback."[7] Moreover, topographical questions also take into account the importance of routines and repetition—in mathematical terms, the statistical dimension of profiles.

Deleuze, Foucault, and Pierre Bourdieu all give habit (or "habitus") a central place in their work. Bourdieu, like Foucault, has a keen interest in the relationship between systems of classification and social power. For Bourdieu (1984, 170, 172) though, systems of classification are constructed by two simple needs—to differentiate and to account for the practices of taste, as manifested in socioeconomic lifestyles:

> Life-styles are thus the systematic products of habitus, which, perceived in their mutual relations through the schemes of the habitus, become sign systems that are socially qualified (as "distinguished," "vulgar," etc.).

The strength of Bourdieu's "habitus," at least as it relates to this book, lies in its linking of habits and the coding of lifestyle and socioeconomic class. What remains unquestioned, however, is the relationship between coding in other spheres beyond consumption—what I posit as a cybernetic-like system of "reproduction." Indeed, du Gay (du Gay et al. 1997, 100) argues that "[Bourdieu] . . . has little to say about the prior coding of objects in production."

Michel de Certeau refines the discussion of habit within the context of space and place in the city—the so-called art of walking in the city (the pastime of Baudelaire's *flaneur*). As I previously noted, de Certeau has been a central figure in the political-resistance debates in cultural studies. Ironically, discussions of the popular, micropolitical dimensions of everyday life have been largely devoid of any topographical elements. When space has been inserted into the equation, though, the "resistive" agency of the individual remains a fundamental component. Mark Poster's (1997, 124) interpretation of de Certeau, for instance, argues that "The consumer inscribes a pattern into space that was not accounted for in its design." Such moments of resistance, however, are all too often fanciful, individuated, and isolated moments: just as the individual is decentered, so too are the sites of solicitation and feedback. Technologies of solicitation are far more likely to inform and precede the diagramming of space—the designing or mapping of space in response to demographic and psychographic data.

POLITICS BY DEFAULT

Instead of replacing or dismissing the importance of ideological and textual critiques of capitalism, hegemony, governmentality, and consumer culture, in this book I have attempted to highlight the manner in which individuals have become an integral part of the reproduction of consumer markets—through mediated texts in cyberspace and through everyday consumer purchases, queries, rentals, and exchanges. As a consequence, consumer behavior, lifestyles, choices, likes, and dislikes all inform the subsequent production, advertisement, marketing, promotion, and sales of products and services. This cycle of reproduction integrates the consumer within the spheres of production, marketing, and sales, but it rationalizes these spheres and attempts to minimize risks through consumer profiling.

Although sites of solicitation are widespread and topographically dispersed (taking into considering the aforementioned habit, or "habitus"), they nevertheless provide a single technique (or exchange) on which to focus a diagrammatic politics. Whether at a point of sale or at a click on another hypertextual link, the attempt to accumulate information from individuals often relies on a default or otherwise coercive system of automation—the aforementioned rewards and punishments. Computer users, for instance, receive (or download) their browser applications with their cookies activated by default. The economy of personal information on the Web is subsequently governed by an implicitly affirmative technology that by default collects information, tracks the online behavior of users, and punishes those who attempt to maintain control over their personal information and browsing history. Many other computerized consumer exchanges also require individuals to give important demographic information (mainly zip codes or telephone numbers) to make a purchase. Such exchanges, again, are built on technological systems that *by default* require consumers to provide personal information. In addition, mail-order businesses that offer free teasers (such as the CDs and tapes that BMG Music gives away) in exchange for contractual obligations to purchase a number of goods at a relatively high cost also send and bill for products that the consumer has not ordered. BMG's default setting (to buy in absence of an explicit "no thank you") requires consumers to inform the business when they do *not* want a product.

Such default settings are common in a culture that needs to regulate and prioritize a seemingly infinite number of choices, products, and services. However, what consumers, citizens, community groups, and other political organizations need to acknowledge is that under the guise of limiting choices to the easiest, most widely understood, and most "user-friendly" options, default settings serve distinct interests. Computer software giant Microsoft, for example, has captured a sizable portion of the Internet browser market (providing *the* graphic representation of cyberspace) by merely setting their Explorer browser as the default Internet gateway in Windows and in Apple's computer operating systems. In other words, Microsoft has used its PC operating system (Windows) monopoly to "encode" its own browser as a default choice.

Facilitated by default settings, such "genetic monopolies" and other automated "choices"—particularly those that integrate the collection of personal information—have not gone unchallenged by their detractors. The recent antitrust cases brought by the Federal Trade Commission against both Microsoft and Intel are good examples of possible political interventions in a computerized default market that automates and encodes preferred choices for its users.[8]

We are told that the audimeter in the ad is "installed in a
radio receiver in a scientifically selected radio home. By
recording every twist of the dial, every minute of the day
and night, the audimeter obtains precious radio data not
available through any other means." These meters are, of
course, installed with the consent of the scientifically selected
radio owner.

Ethical and social values quite to one side, an instrument of
this sort chimes with a good many other facts of our world.
It is obviously the commercial counterpart of the secret
microphone installed for political reasons. It is the mechanical sleuth which eventually pieces together the radio habits
of a household into a single chart-image. It gives the inside
story, which is typical of X-ray photographs, boudoir journalism, and cubist painting alike. For, as in cubist painting,
the spectator is placed in the center of the picture. (McLuhan
1951, 49–50)

Published in 1951, this excerpt from Marshall McLuhan's *The
Mechanical Bride* provides a fitting conclusion to this book. Mc-
Luhan, the quintessential techno-guru, provides yet another example of market research that has implications far beyond the
switch, dial, or television remote control. His description of the
audimeter speaks to the process of sampling—the use of scientific
methods to patrol, diagnose, and survey particular markets (in this
instance, radio listeners). It reminds us that such techniques collect
very personal information within a space widely respected as being
private. The audimeter is also a technology without an end: it
continuously collects information around the clock. It tracks the
routines and "habits" of listeners, and this information is "charted"

or mapped. Finally, the listener is placed front and center within the picture.

McLuhan's example of the audimeter parallels many points that this book has touched on, particularly the solicitation, diagnosis, and mapping of personal information, but it only hints at the larger ethical and social implications of profiling techniques. Today, however, such profiling techniques are not limited to the home or other institutions; they also litter the paths that we walk down every day of our lives. Moreover, they go beyond attempting to control the quotidian (whether markets or populations) by also attempting to account for the future—probable outcomes, relationships, choices, wants, desires, places, and spaces. As a consequence, media and cultural criticism must begin to challenge not only dominant words, images, and texts but also the techniques and technologies that prescribe, regulate, and provide access to (and control over) political, economic, and cultural forms of power.

1. In this book, the term *economy* refers to the exchange of monetary values and also to symbolic constructs or "linguistic, commercial, sexual, or legal" "symbolic economies" (Goux 1990, 10).

2. The term *cybernetics* was first coined by the mathematician Norbert Wiener in his seminal work entitled *Cybernetics: Or Control and Communication in the Animal and the Machine* (1948). In an attempt to discuss the fundamental elements of cybernetic systems, Wiener (1948, 115) turned to the example of the railroad: "In this system there is a human link in the chain of the transmission and return of information: in what we shall now call the chain of feed-back. It is true that the signalman is not altogether a free agent; that his switches and signals are interlocked, either mechani-

cally or electrically; and that he is not free to choose some of the more disastrous combinations. There are, however, feed-back chains in which no human element intervenes. The ordinary thermostat by which we regulate the heating of a house is one of these."

3. Though a special issue on Innis in an Australian cultural studies journal (Angus & Shoesmith 1993) points to his growing reputation outside North America.

4. Nevertheless, Jean Baudrillard (1994, 1) also recognizes the topographic functions of simulations: "Today abstraction is no longer that of the map, the double, the mirror, or the concept. Simulation is no longer that of a territory, a referential being, or a substance. It is the generation by models of a real without origin or reality: a hyperreal. The territory no longer precedes the map, nor does it survive it. It is nevertheless."

CHAPTER 2

1. Cf. ⟨http://www.anu.edu.au/people/Roger.Clarke⟩.

2. Cf. Elmer (1997a) and (2002) for analyses of Web cookies.

CHAPTER 4

1. For a bibliography of sources on the discriminatory effects of geographical information systems (GISs), see Jon Goss's (1995) excellent discussion of GIS and direct marketing, political campaigns, and credit bureaus.

2. Maxwell (1996b, 107) claims that "interviewers and their supervisors are unique among cultural workers. They are charged with carrying people's life stories across the divide separating two structurally differentiated groups: manufacturers and consumers."

3. Russia has a similar system with twenty-two satellites ("Glonass Nears Full Operation" 1995).

CHAPTER 5

1. See Aniko Bodroughkozy's (2001) discussion of Molson's "Joe Canada" campaign.

2. Although there were no reports of such lengthy expeditions, a documentary of the event, *Invasion of the Beer People* (directed by Albert Nerenberg and produced by George Hargrave for CBC Newsworld), recorded interviews with a number of party crashers who did make their way by various means to the site of the concert.

CHAPTER 6

1. A study from Jupiter Media Metrix indicates that almost 70 percent of U.S. consumers worry that their privacy is at risk online (⟨http://www.

nua.ie/surveys/index.cgi?f=VS&art_id=905358019&rel=true⟩, accessed
June 4, 2002).

2. Refer to ⟨http://xanadu.com.au⟩ for more on Nelson's ideas and the
Xanadu hypertext system.

3. See the Jupiter Media Metrix top 50 Web site rating reports at ⟨http://
www.jmm.com/xp/jmm/press/mediametrixtop50.xml⟩ (accessed June 1,
2001).

4. Computer software programs, including Web browsers, come "pre-
packaged" or "bundled" on PCs with certain settings set at the factory.

5. The problematic of anonymous online identities was a central question
of many early studies of computer-mediated communication.

6. Some three years later (February 1999), Intel's heavily promoted
(online and offline) identification function for its Pentium III chip was
heavily criticized by privacy advocates, spawning the relatively successful
"Big Brother Inside" campaign (a spoof of the corporation's "Intel Inside"
logo). Intel's Web site today (specifically, pages dedicated to the Pentium
III chip) are now devoid of any information about the controversial ID
chip and its accompanying "Web outfitter" service.

7. This address is unique and fixed if the user is on an internal Internet
system (ethernet) or a digital subscriber line (DSL) connection. Any
Internet connection that uses a dial-up (telephone) connection has a random IP address assigned to the user for the duration of the connection.

8. According to the Associated Press ("Agencies Record Web Users'
Habits" 2000), thirteen U.S. government agencies use cookies to track
Internet visitors.

9. In contrast to Netscape, Internet Explorer 4.0 offers its privacy options
under the title "cookie."

10. See Elmer (2001) for a discussion of Tim Berners-Lee and the development of hypertext for the Web.

11. The preferences of Microsoft's products—namely, its Windows operating system and accompanying Explorer Web browser—have served as key points of contention in the ongoing dispute between the corporation and the U.S. Department of Justice.

12. More advanced users, however, hardly receive preferential treatment. A study of Internet users (close to 80 percent of which self-identified as being "Very comfortable" with the Internet) found that while 47 percent of users were concerned enough to change their default cookie preferences, less than 7 percent chose to "Never accept cookies" (GVU WWW Tenth User Survey, ⟨http://www.cc.gatech.edu/gvu/user/survey-1998-10/graphs/use/q81.htm⟩).

CHAPTER 7

1. Former FBI profiler John E. Douglas has become the profiling expert and star of twenty-four-hour television channels such as Fox News and CNN. Douglas (1998, 1999), whose own book titles proclaim his "legendary" status, has forged a media career out of his ability to profile criminal minds and behaviors.

2. Criminal drama programs on television, *Law and Order* or the British mini-series *Cracker*, for example, routinely discuss criminal MOs (or *modus operandi*) to correlate criminal traits to similar patterns from known offenders. Both programs, particularly the latter, also rely on psychological profiling to "get into the mind" of transgressors. Such programming, of course, takes its lead from feature films such as *Silence of the Lambs*, a gruesome crime drama that arguably started the contemporary fascination with the FBI and its criminal behavioral (profiling) unit.

3. Carr (1994) includes the foreword note that "Prior to the twentieth century, persons suffering from mental illness were thought to be "alienated," not only from the rest of society but from their true natures. Those experts were therefore known as alienists."

4. The ACLU have been at the forefront of the argument against the use of racial profiles. In the report "Driving While Black: Racial Profiling on Our Nation's Highways" (Harris 1999), the ACLU recount the first use of racial profiles by law enforcement agencies in the United States:

> The profile, described by one court as "an informally com-
> piled abstract of characteristics thought typical of persons
> carrying illicit drugs," had been used in the war on drugs for
> some time. The first profile was reportedly developed in the
> early 1970s by a Drug Enforcement Administration (DEA)
> Special Agent named Paul Markonni while he was assigned
> to surveillance duty at the Detroit Metropolitan Airport. By
> 1979, Markonni's drug courier profile was in use at over 20
> airports. The characteristics of the Markonni profile were
> behavioral. Did the person appear to be nervous? Did he pay
> for his airline ticket in cash and in large bills? Was he going
> to or arriving from a destination considered a place of origin
> of cocaine, heroin or marijuana? Was he traveling under an
> alias?

> In the 1980s, with the emergence of the crack market, skin
> color alone became a major profile component, and, to an
> increasing extent, black travelers in the nation's airports and
> found themselves the subjects of frequent interrogations and
> suspicionless searches by the DEA and the U.S. Customs
> Service. These law enforcement practices soon spread to
> train stations and bus terminals, as well.

5. One of Hall's (1973) first influential articles at the Birmingham Centre for Contemporary Cultural Studies turned to semiotics to discuss the ideological dimensions of a newspaper photograph.

6. I'm speaking more on a geographical than domestic level—Morley's (1986) work clearly contributes to an understanding of the gendering of space within the home via the consumption of television programming.

7. For some context to the term "Consumer Culture," see Featherstone (1991), Keat and Abercrombie (1994), or Lury (1996).

8. The Department of Justice has since reached an out-of-court agreement with Intel. Microsoft, though, continues to fight the government in the courts. The Associated Press has written a helpful article on the government's allegations of anti-trust against Microsoft. See ⟨http://dailynews.yahoo.com/headlines/ap/technology/story.html?s=v/ap/19990625/tc/microsoft_charges_2.html⟩.

"Agencies Record Web Users' Habits." (2000). *Boston Globe*, October 22, A25.

Altena, Arie. (1999). "The Browser Is Dead; Long Live the Browser." Mediamatic, ⟨http://www.mediamatic.net/cwolk/view/2554⟩ accessed on January 15, 2001.

Alterman, Hyman. (1969). *Counting People: The Census in History*. New York: Harcourt Brace.

Angus, Ian, & Brian Shoesmith (eds.). (1993). "Dependency/Space/ Policy: A Dialogue with Harold A. Innis." *Continuum: The Australian Journal of Media and Culture*, 7(1).

BIBLIOGRAPHY

Appadurai, Arjun. (1990). "Disjuncture and Difference in the Global Cultural Economy." *Theory, Culture, and Society*, 7: 295–310.

Barthes, Roland. (1957). *Mythologies*. Paris: Éditions du Seuil.

"Bass' Titanic Mission." (1996). *Brandweek* (April 29): 18.

Baudrillard, Jean. (1994). *Simulacra and Simulation*. Ann Arbor: University of Michigan Press.

Bauman, Zygmunt. (1988). *Globalization: The Human Consequences*. Oxford: Blackwell.

Beniger, James R. (1986). *The Control Revolution: Technological and Economic Origins of the Information Society*. Cambridge: Harvard University Press.

Bennett, Tony, & Janet Woollacott. (1987). *Bond and Beyond: The Political Career of a Popular Hero*. New York: Metheun.

Bennington, Geoffrey. (1994). *Legislations*. London: Verso.

Bentham, Jeremy. (1995). *The Panopticon Writings*. London: Verso.

Berland, Jody. (1993). "Weathering the North: Climate, Colonialism, and the Mediated Body." In V. Blundell, J. Shepard & I. Taylor (eds.), *Relocating Cultural Studies: Developments in Theory and Research* (pp. 207–225). London: Routledge.

Berners-Lee, Tim. (1999). *Weaving the Web*. New York: HarperBusiness.

Birt, Richard, & Kathy Cooper. (1990). "Bracing for the Coming Sea Change in Marketing." *DM News* (July 30).

Boddy, William. (1999). "Redefining the Home Screen: Technological Convergence as Trauma and Business Plan." Paper presented at the Media in Transition Conference, Massachusetts Institute of Technology, Cambridge, MA, October 8–10, ⟨http://media-in transition.mit.edu/articles/index_boddy.html⟩, accessed on March 1, 2002.

Bodroughkozy, Aniko. (2001). "I ... Am ... Canadian! Examining Popular Culture in Canada: Recent Books." *Topia: A Canadian Journal of Cultural Studies*, 5: 109–118.

Bogard, William. (1996). *The Simulation of Surveillance: Hypercontrol in Telematic Societies*. Cambridge: Cambridge University Press.

Bogue, Ronald. (1991). "Word, Image and Sound: The Non-Representational Semiotics of Gilles Deleuze." In R. Bogue (ed.), *Mimesis in Contemporary Theory* (pp. 77–97). Philadelphia: John Benjamins Press.

Booker, Ellis. (1995). "Labor Day in Tuktoyaktuk." *ComputerWorld*, 29(28): 58.

Bourdieu, Pierre. (1984). *Distinction: A Social Critique of the Judgment of Taste*. Cambridge: Harvard University Press.

Burke, Harry E. (1984). *Handbook of Barcoding Systems*. New York: Van Nostrand Reinhold.

Carey, James W. (1989). *Communication as Culture: Essays on Media and Society*. Boston: Unwin Hyman.

Carr, Caleb. (1994). *The Alienist*. New York: Random House.

Castells, Manuel. (1996). *The Rise of the Network Society*. Oxford: Basil Blackwell.

Causey, James E. (1996). "Molson Ice Promotion to End at North Pole." *Milwaukee Journal Sentinel* (June 24): 3.

Clarke, Roger A. (1988). "Information Technology and Dataveillance." *Communications of the ACM*, 31(5): 498–512.

———. (2001). "Cookies." ⟨http://www.anu.edu.au/people/Roger. Clarke/II/Cookies.html⟩, accessed April 2001.

Cortada, James W. (1996). *Information Technology as Business History: Issues in the History and Management of Computers*. Westport, CT: Greenwood.

Cubitt, Sean. (2000). "The Distinctiveness of Digital Criticism." *Screen*, 41(1): 86–92.

Dandeker, Christopher. (1989). *Surveillance, Power, and Modernity: Bureaucracy and Discipline from 1700 to the Present Day*. New York: St. Martin's Press.

Davies, Jude. (1995). "Gender, Ethnicity, and Cultural Crisis in Falling Down and Groundhog Day." *Screen*, 33(6): 214–232.

Davies, Simon. (1998). "Re-Engineering the Right to Privacy." In P. Agre & M. Rotenberg (eds.), *Technology and Privacy: The New Landscape* (pp. 143–165). Cambridge: MIT Press.

Davis, Stanley. (1987). *Future Perfect*. Reading, MA: Addison-Wesley.

de Certeau, Michel. (1984). *The Practice of Everyday Life*. Berkeley: University of California Press.

Deighton, John, Don Peppers & Martha Rogers. (1994). "Consumer Transaction Databases: Present Status and Prospects." In Robert C. Blattberg, Rashi Glazer & John D. C. Little (eds.), *The Marketing Information Revolution* (pp. 58–79). Boston: Harvard Business School Press.

Deleuze, Gilles. (1986). *Foucault*. Minneapolis: University of Minnesota Press.

———. (1992a). "Postscript on the Societies of Control." *October* 59: 3–7.

———. (1992b). "What Is a Dispositif?" In *Michel Foucault: Philosopher* (pp. 159–168). Trans. Timothy J. Armstrong. London: Routledge.

———. (1993). *The Deleuze Reader*. New York: Columbia University Press.

———. (1995). *Negotiations 1972–1990*. New York: Columbia University Press.

Deleuze, Gilles, & Michel Foucault. (1972). "Les Intellectuels et le Pouvoir." *L'Arc*, 49: 3–10.

Deleuze, Gilles, & Felix Guattari. (1983). *Anti-Oedipus: Capitalism and Schizophrenia*. Minneapolis: University of Minnesota Press.

Douglas, John E., & Mark Olshaker. (1998). *Obsession: The FBI's Legendary Profiler Probes the Psyches of Killers, Rapists, and Stalkers, and Their Victims and Tells How to Fight Back.* New York: Scribner.

———. (1999). *The Anatomy of Motive: The FBI's Legendary Manhunter Explores the Key to Understanding and Catching Violent Criminals.* New York: Scribner.

"Dry Ice." *Advertising Age* (February 14): 20.

du Gay, Paul, Stuart Hall, Linda James, Hugh Mackay & Keith Nagus. (1997). *Doing Cultural Studies: The Story of the Sony Walkman.* London: Sage.

Elmer, Greg. (1997a). "Spaces of Surveillance: Indexicality and Solicitation on the Internet." *Critical Studies in Mass Communication*, 14(2): 182–191.

———. (1997b) "The X-Files and Profiles of Canadian Landscape." *Borderlines*, 44: 6–9.

———. (2001). "Hypertext on the Web: The Beginning and End of Web Path-ology." *Space and Culture*, 10: 1–14.

———. (2002). "The Case of Web Browser Cookies: Enabling/Disabling Convenience and Relevance on the Web." In G. Elmer (ed.), *Critical Perspectives on the Internet* (pp. 49–62). Boulder: Rowman and Littlefield.

Featherstone, Mike. (1991). *Consumer Culture and Postmodernism.* London: Sage.

Feschuk, Scott. (1995a). "Arctic Concert Goers Pumped for Polarpalooza." *Globe and Mail* (September 2): A1.

———. (1995b). "Love in No Condition to Charm Northern Fans." *Globe and Mail* (September 4): C3.

Fiske, John. (1989a). *Reading the Popular*. London: Routledge.

———. (1989b). *Understanding Popular Culture*. Boston: Unwin Hyman.

———. (1992). "Cultural Studies and the Culture of Everyday Life." In L. Grossberg, C. Nelson & P. Treichler (eds.), *Cultural Studies* (pp. 154–173). London: Routledge.

———. (1993). *Power Plays, Power Works*. London: Verso.

Foucault, Michel. (1965). *Madness and Civilization: A History of Insanity in the Age of Reason*. New York: Random House.

———. (1973). *The Birth of the Clinic: An Archaeology of Medical Perception*. New York: Vintage.

———. (1977). *Discipline and Punish: The Birth of the Prison*. New York: Vintage.

———. (1978). *The History of Sexuality: An Introduction*. New York: Randon House.

———. (1980). *Power/Knowledge: Selected Interviews and Other Writings, 1972–1977*. New York: Pantheon.

———. (1986). "Of Other Spaces." *Diacritics*, 16(1): 22–27.

Gabriel, John. (1996). "What Do You Do When Minority Means You? Falling Down and the Construction of 'Whiteness.'" *Screen*, 37(2): 129–152.

Gallagher, Kathleen. (1996). "Catalina Is Right On Target with Coupon Marketing." *Milwaukee Journal Sentinel*, August 5, 7.

Gandy, Oscar H. (1993). *The Panopticon Sort: A Political Economy of Personal Information*. Boulder: Westview Press.

————. (1995). "It's Discrimination, Stupid!" In James Brook & Iain Boal (eds.), *Resisting the Virtual Life: The Culture and Politics of Information* (pp. 35–47). San Francisco: City Lights.

Genosko, Gary. (1996). "Introduction." In G. Genosko (ed.), *The Guattari Reader*. Oxford: Basil Blackwell.

Gilbert, Faye W., & William E. Warren. (1995). "Psychographic Constructs and Demographic Segments." *Psychology and Marketing*, 12(3): 223–237.

"Glonass Nears Full Operation." (1995). *Aviation Week and Space Technology*, 143(15): 52–53.

Goldman, Robert, & Stephen Parson. (1994). "Advertising in the Age of Hypersignification." *Theory, Culture, and Society*, 11: 23–53.

Gordon, Charles. (1993). "Hey, Get Your Ice-Hot Beer Here!" *Maclean's* (June 14): 9.

Goss, Jon. (1995). "We Know Who You Are and We Know Where You Live: The Instrumental Rationality of Geodemographic Systems." *Economic Geography*, 71(2): 171–199.

Goux, Jean Joseph. (1990). *Symbolic Economies: After Marx and Freud*. Ithaca: Cornell University Press.

Guattari, Felix. (1977). *Molecular Revolutions: Psychiatry and Politics*. New York: Penguin.

————. (1995). *Chaosmosis: An Ethico-Aesthetic Paradigm*. Bloomington: Indiana University Press.

Hacking, Ian. (1990). *The Taming of Chance*. Cambridge: Cambridge University Press.

Halacy, Dan. (1980). *Census: One Hundred Ninety Years of Counting America*. New York: Elsevier/Nelson.

Hall, Stuart. (1973). "The Determinations of News Photographs." In Stanley Cohen and Jock Young (eds.), *The Manufacture of News: Deviance, Social Problems and the Mass Media*. London: Constable.

————. (1980). "Encoding/Decoding." In Centre for Contemporary Cultural Studies (ed.), *Culture, Media, Language: Working Papers in Cultural Studies, 1972–79*, (pp. 128–138). London: Hutchinson.

Harrell, Gilbert D., Michael D. Hutt & John W. Allen. (1976). *Universal Product Code: Price Removal and Consumer Behavior in Supermarkets*. East Lansing: Michigan State University Press.

Harris, David. (1999). "Driving While Black: Racial Profiling on Our Nation's Highways." Available at ⟨http://aclu.org/profiling/report/index.html⟩, accessed June 1, 2000.

Hart, Christopher W. (1996). "Made to Order: Technology Is Making It Feasible to Reach That Market of One. Make Sure You're the First Mover." *Marketing Management*, 5(2): 10–23.

Harvey, David. (1989). *The Condition of Postmodernity*. Oxford: Basil Blackwell.

Hauser, Philip, & William R. Leonard (eds.). (1946). *Government Statistics for Business Use*. New York: Wiley.

Heyer, Paul. (1995). *Titanic Legacy: Disaster as Media Event and Myth*. Westport, Conn.: Praeger.

Holmlund, Chris. (1991). "Reading Character with a Vengeance: The Fatal Attraction Phenomenon." *Velvet Light Trap*, 27: 25–36.

Ing, David, & Andrew A. Mitchell. (1994). "Point-of-Sale Data in Consumer Goods Marketing: Transforming the Art of Marketing into the

Science of Marketing." In Robert C. Blattberg, Rashi Glazer & John
D. C. Little (eds.), *The Marketing Information Revolution* (pp. 30–57).
Cambridge: Harvard Business School Press.

Innis, Harold. (1951). *The Bias of Communication*. Toronto: University of
Toronto Press.

————. (1972). *Empire and Communications*. Toronto: University of
Toronto Press.

Introna, Lucas, & Helen Nissenbaum. (2000). "The Public Good Vision
of the Internet and the Politics of Search Engines." In Richard Rogers
(ed.), *Preferred Placement: Knowledge Politics on the Web* (pp. 25–47). Maastricht: Jan Van Eyck Akademie Editions.

Jackson, Tim. (1996). "This Bug in Your PC Is a Smart Cookie." *Financial Times*, February 12, 15.

Jackson, Rob. "Close Encounters of the Fourth Kind: A Primer on Customer Contact Marketing." *DM News* (February 1993): 25.

Jackson, Rob, & Paul Wang. (1994). *Strategic Database Marketing*. Lin-
colnwood, IL: NTC Business Books.

Jay, Martin. (1993). *Downcast Eyes: The Denigration of Vision in Twentieth-
Century French Thought*. Berkeley: University of California Press.

Johnson, Richard. (1986). "The Story So Far: And for the Transforma-
tions." In D. Punter (ed.), *Introduction to Contemporary Cultural Studies* (pp.
277–313). London: Longman.

Keat, Russell, & Nicholas Abercrombie (eds.). (1994). *Enterprise Culture*.
London: Routledge.

Landow, George. (1992). *Hypertext: The Convergence of Contemporary Cultural Theory and Technology*. Baltimore: Johns Hopkins Press.

Leach, William. (1993). *Land of Desire: Merchants, Power, and the Rise of a New American Culture*. New York: Pantheon.

Lefebvre, Henri. (1991). *The Production of Space*. Oxford: Basil Blackwell.

Levin, David Michael. (1997). "Keeping Foucault and Derrida in Sight: Panopticism and the Politics of Subversion." In D. M. Levin (ed.), *Sites of Vision: The Discursive Construction of Site in the History of Philosophy* (pp. 397–465). Cambridge: MIT Press.

Loro, Laura. (1995). "Everyone's Talkin' in the 'Multilogue.'" *Advertising Age*, 66(35): 28.

Lull, James. (1990). *Inside Family Viewing: Ethnographic Research on Television's Audiences*. London: Routledge.

Lury, Celia. (1996). *Consumer Culture*. Piscataway, NJ: Rutgers University Press.

Lyon, David. (1994). *The Electronic Eye: The Rise of Surveillance Society*. Minneapolis: University of Minnesota Press.

———. (2001). *Surveillance Society: Monitoring Everyday Life*. Buckingham, UK: Open University Press.

Machlup, Fritz. (1962). *The Production and Distribution of Knowledge in the United States*. Princeton, NJ: Princeton University Press.

Manovich, Lev. (1999). "Database as Symbolic Form." *Convergence: The Journal of Research into New Media Technologies*, 5(2): 80–99.

MapInfo. (1995). "Desktop Mapping: Geocoding." Promotional brochure.

Mapworld. (1996). 1(1): 5.

Marks, John. (1994). "Foucault and Deleuze: Je me Croyais Arrive au Port, et Me Trouvais Rejecte en Pleine Mer." *Renaissance and Modern Studies*, 37: 86–103.

Marsh, Harriet, & Julian Lee. (1996). "Let Good Times Roll to Reach the Youth Market." *Marketing* (May): 16.

Martin, David. (1991). *Geographic Information Systems and Their Socioeconomic Applications*. London: Routledge.

Martin, Geoffrey Lee. (1993). "Cold War on Down Under: Carlton, Tooheys Go Head-to-Head with Summer Brews." *Advertising Age* (December 13): 1–13.

Martin, T. C. (1891). "Counting a Nation by Electricity." *Electrical Engineer*, 12(184): 521–530.

Marx, Karl. (1972). *The Grundrisse*. Ed. and trans. David McLellan. New York: Harper & Row.

Mathieson, Tim. (1997). "The Viewer Society: Michel Foucault's 'Panopticon Revisited.'" *Theoretical Criminology*, 1(2): 215–234.

Mattelart, Armand. (1996). *The Invention of Communication*. Minneapolis: University of Minnesota Press.

Maxwell, Rick. (1996a). "Ethics and Identity in Global Market Research." *Cultural Studies*, 10(2): 238–260.

———. (1996b). "Out of Kindness and into Difference: The Value of Global Market Research." *Media, Culture, and Society*, 18: 105–126.

McLuhan, Marshall. (1951). *The Mechanical Bride: Folklore of Industrial Man*. Boston: Beacon.

Menin, Ben, A. E. Benning & Lee E. Benning. (1992). *The Power of Point-of-Purchase Advertising*. New York: AMACOM.

Michman, Ronald D. (1991). *Lifestyle Market Segmentation*. New York: Praeger.

Miller, Toby. (1997). *Technologies of Truth: Cultural Citizenship and the Popular Media*. Minneapolis: University of Minnesota Press.

Molson Breweries U.S.A. (1995). "From the Land Where Ice Was Born." *Rolling Stone* (advertisement).

Morley, David. (1986). *Family Television: Cultural Power and Domestic Leisure*. London: Comedia.

Mosco, Vincent. (1996). *The Political Economy of Communication*. London: Sage.

Nerenberg, Albert. (1995). *Invasion of the Beer People* (video). Nutaaq Media, Montreal.

NetCarta Corporation. (1996). "A Quick Guide to Internet Spiders, Robots, and Crawlers" [Brochure].

Netscape Communications Corporation. (1995). *1.12 Handbook*.

———. (1996). *3.0 Handbook*.

———. (2000). *6.01 Handbook*.

Nock, Steven. (1993). *The Costs of Privacy: Surveillance and Reputation in America*. New York: Aldine de Gruyter.

Offenhartz, Harvey. (1968). *Point-of-Sale Purchase Design*. New York: Reinhold.

"Outer Limits." (1995). *Newsweek* (June 19): 80.

Parent, Phil, & Larry Konty. (1992). "GIS: Computer Magic Creates the Ultimate Marketing Tool." *Colorado Business Magazine* (July): 20.

Pickles, John. (1995). *Ground Truth: The Social Implications of Geographical*   **165**
Information Systems. London: Guilford.

Poster, Mark. (1990). *The Mode of Information: Poststructuralism and Social
Context*. Chicago: University of Chicago Press.

————. (1991). *The Mode of Information: Poststructuralism and Social Context*. Chicago: University of Chicago Press.

————. (1997). *Cultural History and Postmodernity: Disciplinary Readings
and Challenges*. New York: Columbia University Press.

Pugh, Emerson W., Lyle R. Johnson & John H. Palmer. (1991). *IBM's
360 and Early 370 Systems*. Cambridge: MIT Press.

Randall, Neil. (1997). "The New Cookie Monster: Everyone Is Afraid of
Cookies Lately, but They Can Be Good for You!" *PC Magazine Online*
(April 22), ⟨http://www.zdnet.com/pcmag/issues/1608/pcmg0035htm⟩
accessed on February 15, 2001.

Richtmyer, R. D. (1965). "The Post-War Computer Development."
American Mathematical Monthly, 72(2): 8–14.

Rigdon, Joan E. (1996). "Internet Users Say They'd Rather Not Share
Their Cookies." *Wall Street Journal*, February 14, B6.

Ringle, Ken. (1996). "New Depths for Titanic Promoter: Cruise to Ship
Site Reopens Controversy." *The Washington Post* (August 6): B1, B8.

Robins, Kevin, & Frank Webster. (1988). "Cybernetic Capitalism: Infor-
mation, Technology, and Everyday Life." In Vincent Mosco & Janet
Wasko (eds.), *The Political Economy of Information* (pp. 44–75). Madison:
University of Wisconsin Press.

Rodowick, D. N. (1990). "Reading the Figural." *Camera Obscura*, 24:
11–46.

Rundles, Jeff. (1992). "A GIS Pioneer in Colorado." *Colorado Business Magazine* (July): 40.

Saunders, Michael. (1995). "Marketing in the Arctic: Call It Tuk Rock." *Boston Globe* (September 2): 25.

Shields, Rob. (2000). "The Ethic of the Index and Its Space-Time Effects." In Andrew Herman & Thomas Swiss (eds.), *The World Wide Web and Contemporary Cultural Theory* (pp. 145–160). London: Routledge.

Soja, Edward. (1989). *Postmodern Geographies: The Reassertion of Space in Critical Social Theory*. Oxford: Blackwell.

———. (1996). *Thirdspace: Journeys to Los Angeles and Other Real-and-Imagined Places*. Oxford: Basil Blackwell.

Sorkin, M. (1992). "See You in Disneyland." In M. Sorkin (ed.), *Variations on a Themepark: The New American City and the End of Public Space* (pp. 205–232). New York: Hill & Wang.

Sunstein, Cass. (2001). *Republic.com*. Princeton: Princeton University Press.

"Temperatures Rising on Ice Beer Ads." (1994). *Advertising Age* (February 28): 2.

TiVo Inc. (2001). White Paper submitted to the Federal Trade Commission, ⟨www.tivo/support/site_privacy.asp?frames=no⟩, accessed September 2002.

Tomas, David. (1995). "Feedback and Cybernetics: Reimagining the Body in the Age of Cybernetics." In Mike Featherstone & Roger Burrows (eds.), *Cyberspace, Cyberbodies, Cyberpunk: Cultures of Technological Embodiment* (pp. 21–43). London: Sage.

Tulloch, John, & Manuel Alvarado. (1983). *Doctor Who: The Unfolding Text*. New York: St. Martin's Press.

Urry, John. (1995). *Consuming Places*. London: Routledge.

U.S. Department of Energy. (1998). *I-034: Internet Cookies*. Computer Incident Advisory Center, March 12, ⟨http://www.ciac.org/bulletins/i-034.shtml⟩, accessed May 2001.

Wakeford, Nina. (2000). "New Media, New Methodologies: Studying the Web." In D. Gauntlett (ed.), *Web Studies: Rewiring Media Studies for the Digital Age* (pp. 31–41). London: Arnold.

Warner, Fara. (1994). "Inventive Events Marketers Cutting a Grassroots Edge." *Brandweek*, 35(4): 18–20.

Webster, Frank. (1995). *Theories of the Information Society*. London: Routledge.

Wernick, Andrew. (1991). *Promotional Culture: Advertising, Ideology, and Symbolic Expression*. London: Sage.

Whalen, David. 2001. *The Unofficial Cookie FAQ, Version 2.54.* ⟨http://www.cookiecentral.com/faq⟩, accessed March 2001.

Whitaker, Reg. (1999). *The End of Privacy: How Total Surveillance Is Becoming a Reality*. New York: New Press.

Wiener, Norbert. (1948). *Cybernetics: Or Control and Communication in the Animal and the Machine*. New York: Technology Press.

Williams, Raymond. (1974). *Television: Technology and Cultural Form*. Glasgow: Fontana Press.

Wilson-Smith, Anthony. (1996). "That Sinking Feeling: Salvagers Fail to Raise a Piece of the Fabled Titanic." *Maclean's* (September 9): 16–17.

Wood, Denis. (1992). *The Power of Maps*. New York: Guildford.

Woods, Shirley E. Jr. (1983). *The Molson Saga, 1793–1983*. Toronto: Doubleday.

Woodside, Arch G. (1994). "Modeling Linkage Advertising: Going Beyond Better Media Comparisons." *Journal of Advertising Research* (July/ August): 22–32.

INDEX